Solve Common Teaching Challenges in Children with Autism

TOPICS IN AUTISM

Solve Common Teaching Challenges in Children with Autism

8 ESSENTIAL STRATEGIES FOR PROFESSIONALS & PARENTS

Edited by Lara Delmolino, Ph.D., BCBA-D

Sandra L. Harris, Ph.D., series editor

Woodbine House

All rights reserved. Published in the United States of America by Woodbine House, Inc., 6510 Bells Mill Road, Bethesda, MD 21702. 800-843-7323. www.woodbine-house.com.

Library of Congress Cataloging-in-Publication Data

Solve common teaching challenges in children with autism : 8 essential strategies for professionals & parents / edited by Lara Delmolino.
    pages cm
  Includes bibliographical references and index.
  ISBN 978-1-60613-253-1 (pbk.) -- ISBN 978-1-60613-254-8 (ebook) 1. Autistic children--Education. I. Delmolino, Lara.
  LC4717.S658 2015
  371.9--dc23
                                                                    2014050120

Manufactured in the United States of America
First edition

10   9   8   7   6   5   4   3   2   1

To our mentor and inspiration, Sandra Harris,
without whom the DDDC and its accomplishments would not exist.
We share a deep appreciation for her role in establishing
and maintaining the DDDC as an environment that values science,
compassion, generosity, and excellence.

Table of Contents

Acknowledgments

The authors wish to thank their DDDC colleagues, Marlene Brown, Barbara Kristoff, Donna Sloan, and Todd Frischmann, who contributed to the content and compilation of ideas in this book.

We are grateful to the children and adults with ASD and their families who trust the DDDC with their loved ones and collaborate with us to achieve the best possible outcomes for the people we serve. We appreciate our school district and consultative partners, who help us continue to understand the nuances of adapting and implementing strategies outside of specialized settings.

Finally the authors commend and thank the DDDC staff, who work tirelessly to deliver the best intervention possible and strive for growth and excellence every day.

Introduction
Lara Delmolino

Why This Book?

The short answer is that we, the authors, have noticed that many of the best-intentioned educators tend to make similar mistakes when teaching learners with autism spectrum disorders (ASD). We hope to provide instructors with a guide that will help them avoid these common pitfalls so they can focus on improving the effectiveness of their teaching strategies—many of which are already in place, but simply need to be fine-tuned.

Why Is It Difficult to Teach Children with ASD?

The education and treatment of children with ASD is an ever-changing field of exploration. Thankfully, decades of clinical work and research studies have set the foundation for successful teaching strategies derived from the field of applied behavior analysis (ABA). This field has taught us the importance of analysis—that is, observing, gathering data, and systematically studying the behavior in which we are interested to understand how it is motivated. With a deeper understanding of motivation, we are in a better position to change important behavior and develop critical skills.

We also know that the ASD literature is vast and continues to grow. Each individual with ASD has unique learning and behavior challenges. Although people with ASD share common features, the specific ways they are affected are best understood and addressed at an individual level. We have all heard someone say, "When you have met one person with autism, you've met *one* person with autism."

We understand what a daunting task it can be to stay on top of the growing knowledge about both ASD and ABA. No matter what we know about how to best teach and help people with ASD, there is always something more to learn about how to help *each* person with this diagnosis. As the field unfolds and we develop new, refined, or expanded procedures, practitioners and educators need to continually think about how to adapt, improve, and integrate these new findings.

The current book is an outgrowth of what we see as an inevitable and positive process. People are always learning about the best ways to teach children with autism, and when trained in these strategies, they embrace them and apply them with good intentions and eagerness to improve the lives of their students. But what happens? Everything keeps changing; the clinical research in autism is moving forward at an exciting speed, with each new question inspiring lines of research studies and more exploration. Every year, more articles, books, journals, and conferences are devoted to spreading this information.

What Makes Us Qualified to Write This Book?

The collection of authors who contributed to this book are in a unique position to respond to this state of affairs. Combined, we have decades of experience in both the education of people with autism and the research and dissemination of information about effective teaching strategies. All of us have hands-on experience teaching learners with autism in school, home, and clinic settings. We also have years of experience training and/or advising others how to best teach individuals with autism using the principles and strategies of ABA. A good portion of our collective experience has occurred at the Douglass Developmental Disabilities Center (DDDC), a program that has been dedicated to serving people with autism spectrum disorders at Rutgers, the State University of New Jersey, since 1972. As a university-based program, the DDDC focuses equally on service, training, and scholarship; serving people with autism; training university students, professionals, and the community; and writing and disseminating research and knowledge. In this way, our mission focuses us on the intersection of what is known and what is unknown, and what needs to be questioned further. In our own clinical programs and our consultation services, we recognize that nothing stands still. Recommendations are revised in time; new procedures replace older procedures. Decisions are based on data and outcome, and we continually question what is working, for whom, and why.

A few years ago, our senior faculty and consultation team compiled a list of the most common teaching recommendations we give while training our own staff and during consultation and training in the community. We often saw strategies in place in classrooms and other treatment settings that were informed by good research and that were the result of integrating new findings and information, but that had taken on a life of their own. Some of these strategies and practices had persisted without refinement and needed to be updated or balanced with other perspectives.

Topics Covered in This Book

In the first chapter, Kim Sloman talks about the importance of motivation in teaching, and how we can make sure our teaching is worthwhile for our students. Sometimes, therapists and teachers are applying well-researched strategies to teach a skill without first being able to establish motivation for the child to benefit from the teaching method. In the second chapter, I describe the necessity of harnessing motivation, and balancing the need to teach children to ask for what they want and need while also embedding opportunities for teaching skills that might not be as immediately or obviously rewarding for a child.

In the third chapter, Debra Paone writes about the importance of waiting for the child to attend before beginning a task, as students can only benefit if they are present, engaged, and attending. Her chapter highlights the importance of recognizing and building attending skills, and reminds us that taking the time to wait and build or establish those central skills will make later teaching more successful and meaningful.

In chapter 4, Ben Thomas discusses a related issue: the use of manual guidance, or teaching by using your hands to guide a child through a lesson or task. Ben describes the effective use of manual guidance while remaining alert to see if manual guidance is being used in ways that may actually inhibit students' learning and independence.

Sometimes we have seen excessive physical guidance used as a way to teach when a student does not have enough motivation, attending, or other foundation skills to work from.

Kate Fiske addresses how teachers use language in her chapter. She describes a phenomenon we have seen in classrooms: a language-rich environment that inadvertently dilutes the meaningful use of language, making it harder for children to attend to and learn from the teacher's narrative. She describes ways for instructors to develop insight into their use of language with their students and to think strategically.

In chapter 6, Catriona Francis focuses on the importance of balancing the quality of intervention with the quantity of services. She tackles the fundamental question of how to best evaluate intensity of treatment, and whether it can be something that is counted in trials or hours. She commends practitioners who strive for many and frequent learning opportunities, but cautions about the need to monitor quality and not sacrifice quality for quantity. That error is something we have all seen in classrooms and home programs.

The final two chapters remind educators and parents to focus on the needs of each individual child, and recognize how sometimes thinking generally about "people with autism" prevents more individualized and meaningful practices. In chapter 7, Robert LaRue describes the concept of individualization and how teaching goals and methods may need to be assessed and tailored to the learner in order to be most effective for a specific person. In the final chapter, Maria Arnold discusses the importance of making decisions that are meaningful for each person, for his or her immediate and future life experiences. This perspective, and the planning that must accompany it, is important components to reflect on throughout a child's educational experience and on a regular basis.

The common theme throughout the book, and in our collective experience, is that these teaching challenges are not unique. These situations develop when dedicated and motivated instructors or caregivers are doing what they need to do—they are involved and active in teaching and are working to apply methods they have learned or strategies developed from their own experience. Our universal caution, then, is to always stop, take a step back, and rethink what you are doing and why. We end each of the chapters with a checklist to guide you through this self-assessment process, and to help you gain insight about why your current methods may not be working or why you—and the learner—may be getting stuck. Developing insight and a way to recognize the need to make revisions is essential to being as effective an instructor as possible.

1 | Make It Worthwhile

Kimberly Sloman

Sally is an eight-year-old girl with ASD who receives ABA instruction in a self-contained classroom. "We have a very difficult time keeping Sally on-task," states Sally's teacher, Mrs. Stuart. "Sally engages in really high rates of repetitive, stereotypic motor behavior like tapping, hand flapping, and body rocking throughout her work sessions. She has a few favorite foods but seems to tire of them easily. Sometimes she'll ask for popcorn, but when we try to have her work for it, she stops paying attention or starts engaging in motor stereotypy. It's like it's not worth it for her to do the work."

When asked about other items or activities Sally may like, Mrs. Stuart reports, "Sally's not really interested in any of the activities the classroom has to offer. If she does engage with an item, it is usually accompanied by the repetitive tapping. We've tried presenting her with videos on the iPad, but she usually ignores the video and taps at the screen. We're really struggling to find a way to motivate her."

Mrs. Stuart is facing a common problem in instructing individuals with ASD: she and her fellow teachers just cannot seem to engage Sally in the classroom activities that are essential for her learning. In contrast, typically developing students usually comply with academic demands to get access to more naturalistic reinforcers. That is, they work hard in school to receive praise from parents and teachers or to avoid reprimands or other negative consequences (e.g., being "grounded"). They are also often motivated by delayed outcomes from completing academic tasks such as getting good grades, getting into college, or benefitting from increased job opportunities. However, oftentimes students with ASD require additional motivation to respond. Teachers and parents need to know not only what items and activities are reinforcing for their students or children but also how to use them effectively to maximize each child's potential.

Overview of the Issue: Reinforcement and Motivation

Every day we all respond to people and events in our environment with behaviors we have learned. We use those behaviors because they have received reinforcement in the past. Reinforcement is the process by which a certain behavior becomes more likely to occur due to the environmental consequences of that behavior. That is, we are more likely to repeat responses that are followed by pleasant events or the removal of unpleasant events.

Any event that follows a person's behavior and results in that person using the behavior more often is a *reinforcer*. A *positive reinforcer* is any event that is presented following a behavior that increases behavior. For example, we may choose to wear a particular shirt because in the past our friends have complimented us on how it looks. In this case, the compliment is a positive reinforcer for the behavior of wearing the shirt. A *negative reinforcer* is any event that increases behavior when it is removed. For example, we may quickly put folded laundry in the basket away because we know our spouse will then stop scowling at us. The scowl is a type of (negative) reinforcer because escaping it increases our behavior (putting away the laundry).

Clearly, the consequences that follow behavior play an integral role in the future occurrence of behavior. However, in order for those consequences to be effective for any given person, that person must be motivated to receive those consequences. In other words, we have to find certain events desirable in order for them to be reinforcing to us. Motivating operations (MOs) are events that alter the effectiveness of reinforcers. Using the above example of "shirt wearing," some responses (MOs) are more likely to motivate us to wear the shirt than others. For instance, a possible MO for the compliment is whether or not we like the person delivering it. If we are given a compliment on our shirt by someone we do not particularly like or want to interact with, the compliment will not function as a reinforcer. We will not be any more likely to wear that shirt in the future (we may possibly be less likely to wear it). Likewise, if we don't mind having our spouse scowl at us, we will not be motivated to remove the scowl by putting away laundry. Motivation is complex and may be affected by several different factors. Generally, if we are rewarded with a particular reinforcer too frequently, the reinforcer will become less effective. When we are "deprived" of certain events, they are more effective as reinforcers. Perhaps pizza is your favorite food. You may be more likely to order a pizza if it has been several weeks since you last ate it. The act of ordering a pizza is reinforced when the delivery man arrives at your door with a piping hot pepperoni pie. However, the chances of you making that call decrease if you've just been to an "all-you-can-eat" buffet. Your extended access to other food and "being full" has decreased your motivation to get pizza. Likewise, if you are hungry but have eaten pizza for lunch and dinner the previous five days, your motivation for that particular reinforcer may be low.

Adding to the complexity of motivation is the fact that several MOs are acting on each of us at any given time. We may be motivated to get food, sleep, finish chores, talk to a friend, watch a TV show, or complete a work task all at the same time. Therefore, motivation for a particular event (getting food) may be affected by the motivation for other events. For example, we may not make the call to order a pizza because motivation to finish cleaning the house takes precedence.

Reinforcement and Motivation for Learners with ASD

The behaviors of learners with ASD also occur because of a history of reinforcement. Like anybody else, people with ASD will engage in behavior that results in access to preferred items and activities and avoidance of nonpreferred events.

To motivate individuals with ASD to learn important academic and life skills, teachers and parents provide reinforcers (preferred items or activities) following desired behavior. We know that the reinforcement process has worked when the student is able to correctly use those desired behaviors in a variety of situations. However, there are several challenges inherent in ASD that affect the learner's preferences and how she responds to certain consequences:

First, people with ASD may be less sensitive to social attention as a consequence for their behavior. They may not be motivated by receiving praise and may also be resistant to interacting with others, even to meet basic wants and needs (such as by approaching an adult to get a favorite food).

Second, individuals with ASD often have language deficits. This may make it more difficult to determine their preferences because they may not be able to vocally tell us what they do and do not like.

Third, these learners also may be less sensitive to delayed consequences, or having to wait to receive a reward after performing a response. As a result, delayed consequences may be ineffective as reinforcers for individuals with ASD.

Fourth, learners with ASD are more likely to have restricted interests. That is, they may only be motivated to interact with one item or to discuss one particular subject. As a result, they may react negatively to the introduction of new items or activities.

Fifth, learners with ASD are likely to engage in repetitive behavior. Often this behavior serves a self-stimulatory function and is done for nonsocial reasons. In other words, the individual finds the behavior itself reinforcing and is motivated to engage in it regardless of others' reactions.

Taken together, characteristics of ASD along with the complex nature of reinforcement and motivation can make it difficult to effectively teach students with ASD. If we cannot identify consistently effective ways to motivate our students, their academic progress may suffer, and they may begin to engage in other forms of inappropriate behavior.

What Do Problems with Motivation Look Like?

A lack of motivation can present itself in several forms:
- You may notice a lack of motivation in how your child or student interacts with the people or objects in her environment. Some children may not approach or engage with any items they are presented with. Others may briefly show interest in an item but tire of it quickly.
- You may notice that your child's interest in an item changes as the work session goes on.
- Some children may interact with items when the response

effort is low (all they have to do is reach for something they like) but will not perform a task to gain access to the items.

■ Some students might have competing responses that negatively affect motivation for the activities we are trying to use as reinforcers. Common competing responses include off-task, self-stimulatory, or problem behaviors, which are described in more detail below.

- Some individuals might display inattention or off-task behavior. That is, they might seem distracted or more interested in their surroundings than task materials (for example, turning away from task materials or looking around the room).

- Other children might engage in self-stimulatory behavior. For example, for Sally, described above, her motivation to engage in motor stereotypy may have competed with motivation to remain on task.

- Sometimes, motivation to engage in other forms of problem behavior may compete with the appropriate behavior you are trying to teach. For example, a student may engage in disruptive behavior to receive attention. Her motivation to engage in the disruptive behavior may outweigh her motivation to complete math problems in order to be rewarded with an independent activity she enjoys such as reading books.

In each of these examples, if the learner's motivation for academic behavior is not present or compromised, it will not be possible to reinforce the important skills you are trying to teach her.

Where Do Problems with Motivation Come From and What Can We Do about It?

Several factors may contribute to the problems with motivation described above. A primary problem may be difficulty identifying preferred items or activities for the child or student. However, even if you have identified potential reinforcers, there are other possible issues that can contribute to problems with motivation including satiation, ratio strain, and competing responses.

Reinforcer Identification

What's the Problem?

One factor related to motivation may be problems with identifying reinforcers for our students. We should not assume items are reinforcers because they have been successful for another student. Reinforcers should be individually assessed. We should also not assume that a child will continue to enjoy certain items or activities just because they were successfully used in the past. Preferences change, and our students may not enjoy the same items they did several months or even days ago. Another potential problem is relying on others to tell us what a student enjoys rather than directly observing her ourselves. Verbal reports may be a good starting point but should always be supplemented with more structured preference assessments using direct observation measures.

What Can We Do about It?

Several structured, effective methods are available to assess an individual's preferences, and numerous research articles support the use of these types of preference assessments for individuals with ASD. Though the methods will only be briefly described here, several published reviews of the literature exist (e.g., Tullis et al., 2011). You can also read more about several specific methods of assessing preference in the appendix to this book. All methods can use a variety of foods (based upon parent report) and toys (e.g., puzzles; cause and effect, music, or light-up toys; sensory bins; computer games; iPads). Commonly used assessment methods include the following:

Single Stimulus Preference Assessment. This method involves presenting one item or activity to the individual at a time and measuring how often she approaches and engages with the item. For example, the teacher may place a water bin in front of a child to see if she will reach for and interact with the items in the water. The single stimulus method provides information on whether the individual is interested in a particular item but does not allow for comparisons between items, as the other methods do.

Paired-Choice Preference Assessment. This method involves repeatedly presenting the individual with two items at the same time and noting which items she selects most to identify relative preference between the items. For example, the therapist may select five to seven items or activities to include based on her parents' suggestions. Each item is paired with every other item at least one time. For instance, the therapist presents two activities (coloring book and iPad) to the learner and gives her the choice to "pick one." Once she states her choice or points to the activity, she is briefly allowed to do the activity or play with the item. The therapist notes how often an activity is selected. In this case, the activities that are consistently selected are considered potential reinforcers.

Multiple Stimulus without Replacement Assessment. In MSWO preference assessments, a number of activities and items the student might enjoy are again selected. All items are then presented at the same time, and the learner is allowed to select which one she would most like to use or play with. That item is then removed from the array and the rest of the items are presented. Items are removed from the array, one by one, until all items have been selected by the student. The therapist notes the order the activities were selected, and the activities that are selected first are considered potential reinforcers.

Structured preference assessments are a great starting point for helping us identify items or activities our students may like. However, in each of the above preference assessment formats, the target behavior is prompted by the therapist (items are presented and the student is sometimes told "Pick one"). In addition, the target response is simply approaching the item or activity.

It may be useful to conduct more naturalistic observations in an enriched environment in which several different activities and items are available to observe what the learner prefers to do in the absence of prearranged options. This type of assessment could provide important information about which types of activities attract your child or student, how she interacts with the items, and how long she remains actively engaged. It could also provide information on whether she prefers to engage in potential competing responses (such as stereotypy) rather than engage with the items.

Satiation

What's the Problem?

Satiation occurs when extended time with an item or activity decreases its effectiveness as a reinforcer. Satiation is a natural part of our daily lives. We sit down for a meal when we are hungry and stop eating when we feel full (or satiated). We may enjoy the company of others for several hours and then find ourselves less interested in conversation topics.

When students with ASD have had enough of a particular reinforcer, no matter how much it appealed to them at one time, they too are satiated. When this happens, we are often left with no effective way to motivate them to engage in appropriate behavior. Satiation may be more likely to occur in individuals with ASD who have restricted interests. Since they have few identified interests, similar items are used over and over again to motivate them. Satiation may also occur when students have access to items or activities used as reinforcers outside of teaching sessions or receive reinforcement for responses that take minimal effort (i.e., it is too easy for them to obtain the reinforcer).

What Can We Do about It?

The problem of satiation can be avoided from several angles. First, we should be evaluating how we are providing access to a particular reinforcer. We know that time away from items can increase motivation for those items. Thus, to the extent possible, caregivers should limit their children's access to reinforcers outside of the work session. If coloring books are a highly preferred activity, make sure that coloring books are only available during work sessions.

If satiation is a problem, we also need to evaluate how we are delivering reinforcers. It is possible that we are providing too much access during the work session and that lessening access to reinforcers (e.g., shorter duration of time with the iPad, smaller pieces of food) would improve the student's motivation during the session. Similarly, increasing the schedule of reinforcement (e.g., number of responses required to gain access to a reinforcer) may also help avoid satiation. For example, you might intermittently reinforce the student's appropriate responses and compliance with demands (on average after every five responses) rather than after every response. However, it is important to provide your child or student with enough access to the things she enjoys to effectively promote skills. Not providing enough access to reinforcement can result in other problems related to motivation (see the section on Ratio Strain below).

It may be possible to decrease satiation by using varied and novel items and activities within the work session. You should rotate access to the items throughout the session so that the same item is not used repeatedly. If you have a learner with a limited catalog of appropriate reinforcers, it may be time to get creative and think outside the box. Channel your inner *MacGyver!* You have a piece of string, a tongue depressor, and sixteen cotton balls—make a reinforcer! In all seriousness, our learners may need new and imaginative ways to interact with items. They may not enjoy coloring on a flat surface but may like to color over different textures. Matchbox cars rolling across the desk might not pique their interest but a race track with steep drops might.

If inappropriate behavior seems to be competing with a child's ability to engage appropriately with objects and activities, try to direct her inappropriate behavior to more appropriate forms. For example, does the student enjoy splashing in the bathroom sink? If so, you might create a water play station for her. Does she like tapping objects? Music toys may provide an appropriate alternative way for her to tap. If she is resistant to novel activities, you may need to gradually introduce her to new activities and reinforce her for engaging with the new activity. For example, you may "pair" or associate the new activity with an established preferred activity. This may involve providing the student with reinforcement when she approaches the new activity and then again when she appropriately interacts with the new activity.

Satiation also may be less likely to occur if generalized conditioned reinforcers are used rather than direct access to preferred items. Generalized conditioned reinforcers are reinforcers that have been paired with a wide variety of other ("backup") reinforcers. Money is an effective generalized conditioned reinforcer for most of us because it can be used to purchase various items and activities we like. Furthermore, it is effective in the absence of any particular MO (money is still effective when we are full from eating).

Praise and tokens are two common generalized conditioned reinforcers that have been effectively used with individuals with ASD. Tokens are small items such as pennies, stickers, or marks on paper that the learner "earns" in return for correct responses. The tokens themselves are initially not reinforcing in and of themselves, but gain effectiveness when the individual exchanges them for items and activities that do have value to her. However, it takes careful planning and fading to establish praise and tokens as reinforcers for which the learner is motivated to work (see Leaf, McEachin & Taubman, 2012 for examples of methods). Briefly, when tokens and praise reliably precede the delivery of established reinforcers, they take on the same qualities as the reinforcers. Because tokens can often be used for a wide variety of different reinforcers, they are less likely to undergo satiation.

Ratio Strain

What's the Problem?

Ratio strain occurs when the demands made on an individual are too high for the amount of reinforcement available to her. Signs of ratio strain include lower levels of responding (or the individual stops responding), increases in emotional behavior, or other inappropriate avoidance behavior. Ratio strain is more likely to occur under situations in which the response requirement is high. However, it also may occur when there is a large increase in the response requirement. For example, suppose a student typically must complete ten math problems to receive reinforcement. If she suddenly needs to complete fifty math problems to obtain the same amount of reinforcement, ratio strain may occur.

Ratio strain is typically used to describe a reaction to the amount of work (number of responses) an individual needs to complete to receive reinforcement. However, similar effects on behavior may occur when the individual is expected to work for long periods of time without reinforcement (duration of work) or when she has to wait extended periods of time after completing the work to access reinforcers (delay to reinforcement). Additionally, ratio strain may be related to the magnitude or amount of reinforcement. For example, you may gladly walk ten miles to earn $1,000. However, if walking ten miles only earns you $5, you are less likely to engage in the behavior. Likewise, our students may be less likely to comply with difficult demands if the amount of reinforcement is small (twenty seconds with a preferred toy or a tiny piece of chip).

What Can We Do about It?

The amount of and type of work a student is asked to do should always be individually determined. First and foremost, we should ensure that the student has the appropriate prerequisite skills to complete the tasks we are asking of her. We need to make sure we are setting her up for success by providing programming that suits her specific educational needs.

Just as programming should be customized, the amount of work and time spent working should also be tailored to each child. Some students may require more frequent and immediate reinforcement, while others are able to work for extended periods of time with no problems. However, if motivation is a potential issue and a student is engaging in off-task behavior, it may be because the work requirements are too high.

Because ratio strain is more likely to occur when response requirements are increased rapidly, you may avoid this problem by *gradually* increasing work requirements (both amount of work and time spent working) for your child or student. For new or difficult tasks, it is best to begin with high levels of reinforcement (providing reinforcement after she has performed one task correctly, or has been on-task for one minute) and then space out or delay reinforcer delivery. Increasing the amount of work required slowly and systematically will teach her to tolerate more and more work for less reinforcement.

Ratio strain may also be avoided by ensuring that the amount of work you are asking your students to do matches the amount of reinforcement you are providing. There has to be a careful balance between providing enough reinforcement to make engaging in the task worthwhile while at the same time preventing possible satiation from occurring. At times, teachers and caregivers may feel that increasing the levels of reinforcement takes away from learning opportunities (e.g., the student is spending extended time playing with the iPad and not engaged with instruction). However, more reinforcement may result in higher quality responses and more time on task in the long run. See chapter 6, "Quality over Quantity," for more discussion of this balance.

Competing Responses

What's the Problem?

Competing responses are other forms of behavior that are interfering with the skills we are trying to teach. That is, the MO for these competing responses is stronger than the MO for the reinforcers we are providing. For Sally, the motivation to engage in hand flapping and other repetitive movements appeared to compete with her motivation to do academic tasks. That is, she would rather flap her hands for self-stimulation than work for the reinforcers the class was providing. For other students, the motivation to escape a difficult task may compete with the motivation to complete the task. For example, a student may engage in disruptive behavior such as swiping materials and flopping on the floor because the reinforcers for completing the task are too small or too delayed. These competing responses prevent adults from effectively reinforcing target skills.

What Can We Do about It?

We can prevent competing responses by first identifying highly preferred reinforcers for the learner and then ensuring that we only provide them to her after "clean" target responses. That means that you should only deliver reinforcement for a correct response that occurs without any other inappropriate behavior. In other words, make sure that your child or student with ASD is not having her cake and eating it too. For example, your student cannot engage in stereotypy throughout a work activity and still earn reinforcement.

Once you are sure that you are reserving your identified reinforcers for appropriate responding, you may also need to minimize other forms of reinforcement for inappropriate behavior. (Functional behavior assessments may be necessary to identify the causes of inappropriate behavior.) For example, if you notice that the student is able to avoid tasks and receive extra attention for disruptive behavior, you may need to reduce the time she is able to avoid tasks and ensure she does not receive attention following disruptive behavior. You can then also "stack the deck" in favor of appropriate behavior by providing enriched breaks with preferred items and attention following appropriate behavior.

In another situation, you may notice that there is typically a delay in reinforcement following an appropriate request (the individual has to wait two minutes), but she gets something she wants more immediately following inappropriate behavior. In this case, you should work to decrease the delay to reinforcement and perhaps let the student have more time with her reinforcers following appropriate requests to decrease her motivation to engage in inappropriate behavior.

People with ASD often persist in stereotypy due to nonsocial consequences or the stimulation the behavior itself provides. For that reason, if stereotypy is a competing response, it may be more difficult to address. However, numerous published studies have shown that stereotyped behavior can be successfully treated. In some cases, it may be possible to use highly potent items and activities to reinforce the individual for not engaging in stereotypy. For example, a child may earn something she really likes (e.g., her favorite kind of candy) for not repetitively tapping objects for five minutes.

It may also be possible to identify items or activities that compete with stereotypy but that do not interfere with work tasks. For example, if the student often engages in noncontextual speech (e.g., repeating lines from videos she has seen in the past), you might be able to provide competing activities such as playing soft background music during work to decrease vocal stereotypy. When you use competing activities, you need to conduct direct assessments to ensure that the activities do not also compete with motivation to work.

If powerful reinforcers or competing activities cannot be identified, you may need to use other procedures to teach the learner when stereotypy is permitted. For example, you might use minimal physical redirection to block a child from engaging in certain forms of stereotypy during work tasks but allow her to engage in the behavior in certain areas of the classroom or home or when she has breaks from work tasks.

Summing Up

In order for reinforcement to be effective with students with ASD, the students must have motivation to obtain those reinforcers. However, everyone's motivation is constantly changing and is affected by a number of factors, including time spent with a certain reinforcer, the effort required to complete the behavior, amount of reinforcement provided, and competing responses.

Individuals with ASD often present other challenges that complicate our ability to effectively motivate them. Using direct preference assessment methods will help us identify potential reinforcers and increase the variety of reinforcers used in work sessions. Parents and instructors should strive to be creative and expand the reinforcer repertoire of their children or students. In some cases, providing direct reinforcement to individuals for approaching and interacting with new items and activities may be necessary. Using novel activities and avoiding extended periods of time with the same items will help to avoid the problem of satiation and keep our learners motivated to learn. We can also keep children more motivated by individualizing the amount and type of work required and gradually increasing response requirements over time. If we suspect that other inappropriate behavior such as disruptive behavior or stereotypy is interfering with a student's ability to learn, we should work to minimize reinforcement of those responses and maximize reinforcement for appropriate target skills. Doing so will ensure that we are getting the most out of our reinforcers and making the student's effort worthwhile.

SELF-ASSESSMENT: Are You "Making It Worthwhile?"

Observe teaching interactions within the classroom and respond to the following questions:

1. What skill is being targeted? _____

2. What is being used to motivate the student?

   _____

3. Does the learner appear motivated? _____

   ■ Does the student engage with any items?

   _____

   ■ Does the intended motivating item or activity work briefly, but then lose its potency?

   _____

   ■ Does the student select an item but not seem to want it?

   _____

   ■ Does anything seem to compete with stereotypy?

   _____

4. How was the student's motivation/preference assessed?

   _____

5. Could any of the following be factors in the current scenario?

   ❑ Just because the student approaches an item does not mean it serves as a reinforcer.

   ❑ The student has gotten used to the items we have.

   ❑ The same items are used over and over again.

   ❑ The student has too much free access.

   ❑ The student has to put in too much effort to get the item (it's not worth it; the student has to work for a long time (e.g., 15 minutes) for a crumb of a food reward).

6. What are possible solutions to #5?

_____

_____

_____

7. What is the student doing (what does he or she often do)?
   How could this be channeled into more appropriate behavior?

_____

_____

_____

8. What novel items could be introduced? What creative ways to
   interact with items could be introduced?

_____

_____

_____

9. How can you stack the deck in favor of appropriate behavior?

   ☐ Quality of reinforcer

   ☐ Quantity of reinforcer (schedule, duration)

   ☐ Delay access to the reinforcer

   ☐ Ratio strain (amount of work to reinforcer access)

2 | Don't Give It Away

Lara Delmolino

Lucy and Tom Evans remembered how important it was to focus on motivating Charlie to learn. When Charlie had first begun participating in early intervention sessions in their home, the therapist had worked with Lucy and Tom to build learning opportunities into their everyday interactions with Charlie. One of the most important ways they learned to do this was by helping Charlie learn to mand for things. In the beginning, the term "mand" was unfamiliar to them. But they soon learned that "mand" was a technical term for requesting, or for Charlie to somehow communicate what he wanted.

Many of Charlie's earliest sessions with his therapist and his parents really focused on helping him indicate what he wanted—so that he could make his "request" and have his therapist or his parents provide what he wanted, to reward the request. For example, Charlie learned to say "uh" when he wanted to be lifted, and to say "puh" when he wanted to be pushed on the swing. In fact, it seemed that his early sessions were spent making very simple requests and getting his requests rewarded.

After months and months of teaching that focused on mand training, Charlie seemed to get the idea! He regularly made specific sounds in these situations to get pushes and to be lifted up. When his therapist Sherrie came to the house, he ran to her because she had always been associated with lots of fun activities. Sherrie talked to Tom and Lucy about this and said that she was glad that her "pairing" had worked. She said that it was very important for Charlie to learn that the teaching environment and everything in it was associated with good things. Now that Charlie seemed to have a positive association with Sherrie and her teaching sessions, it was time to gradually start moving to the next steps.

Sherrie was going to start teaching Lucy and Tom what was next after initial mand training.

Overview of the Issue: Mand Training

Mand training was an important development in the early behavioral intervention for children with ASD. The word "mand" comes from the work of famous psychologist B. F. Skinner, from his book called *Verbal Behavior*. In general, Skinner described all behavior as actions that people learn because the environment responds to their actions in regular and predictable ways. For example, we turn on a light switch because the light usually comes on after we do so. Skinner defined "verbal behavior" as a *type* of behavior that people learn because others around them respond to the actions in regular and specific ways. He differentiated this from "behavior" in general by specifying that "verbal behavior" involved another person; it was "social." In other words, "behavior" produces an effect by acting directly on the environment; "verbal behavior" works by acting on other people, or, "an audience or listener," in Skinner's terms. So, unlike turning on a light switch, which doesn't involve another person, asking someone else to "turn on the light, please" is verbal behavior because the outcome involves the actions of a second person.

Verbal Behavior was a theoretical book, not a practical teaching guide. It was important because Skinner focused on thinking about language the way that psychologists think about other kinds of behavior—how it is learned and how it is maintained. At the time it was published in the 1950s, this was a very new idea—that language followed the same basic laws and principles as other types of behavior that were studied. Skinner's writings encouraged others to think about language by focusing on its functions.

In Skinner's theory, the word "mand" was defined as a behavior that serves the function of specifying or requesting something that the speaker wants. The concept of verbal behavior and how it applies to children with autism is a more extensive topic and one that can be more thoroughly understood by working with a behavior analyst or speech and language professional with training in behavior analysis. For the purposes of this chapter, we are focusing solely on the basic concept of mands and early mand training.

It has always been important to teach children with autism to focus on communication. Teaching children to communicate what they want—to ask for or somehow indicate to a listener that they want something—has been part of behavioral treatment for autism since the beginning. However, in the 1980s, famous clinicians Mark Sundberg and James Partington published a book in which they expressed their view that teachers and therapists should be focusing *more* on the requesting or mand skills of children with autism. Their view was that Skinner's conceptual work and theory of language was not integrated well enough into the general strategies most commonly used for teaching children with autism.

One of the main reasons that Sundberg and Partington recommended changes to teaching procedures was that they had found that some teachers or therapists spent a lot of time teaching children with ASD to respond to teachers' instructions and to respond to other types of teaching procedures, but sometimes did not pay enough attention to teaching the children to initiate interactions. Mand training was introduced as a way to formalize the process of teaching these very important requesting skills.

Mand training was popularized not only to help learners with ASD build very basic early learning skills, but also to help them build motivation for learning in other areas. Increasing the focus on mand training in the field accomplished many needed outcomes. Most importantly, perhaps, mand training can help children with autism spectrum disorders feel more positive about learning. Often, teaching sessions that do not involve manding or mand training may not be naturally motivating, or teaching may occur in places that the child does not prefer. When children with ASD participate in intense intervention, they often experience learning environments as places or situations where they can't engage in the behavior that they might want to engage in, since behavior such as repetitive actions, movements, or play is often interrupted or redirected during intervention. Also, learning environments are filled with demands that may be difficult or unpleasant for people with ASD.

When children have participated in intense intervention that did not focus on mand training or pairing, they may have developed a tendency to avoid work or learning environments. They may protest or avoid the work setting, or engage in problem behavior when asked to begin work or go to a designated work area. For these learners, it will be very important to focus on manding to establish the work setting as a place where rewarding things happen—not just demands.

Mand training is also essential to teaching children with ASD that other people are a source of positive things. When we focus on manding during instruction, it provides many opportunities for children to receive positive things from the person in the environment. Sometimes, the adults in teaching situations are so busy providing instructions and feedback that there are not enough opportunities for the adults to become associated with enjoyable things. Focusing on mand training makes this a priority.

Another important outcome of mand training is that the child has frequent practice in the act of communicating. Since communication is a core deficit for children with ASD, ongoing practice with manding will keep communication as a priority in teaching and increase the chances of positive improvements in communication.

It is often considered good practice to maintain a focus on manding throughout all of the educational opportunities and environments for people with ASD. This is because communication and motivation continue to be challenges when teaching new behaviors and skills throughout a child's life and even into adulthood.

Where Does the Problem Come From?

The problem comes, however, when mand training continues in its most basic form, and is not carefully modified or blended into new learning situations in ways that make sense. Some of the problems that can be seen when mand training continues in this way are discussed below.

Teaching Mands When the Concept of Manding Is Already Acquired

When a child is first participating in mand training, it is important for him to learn that behavior or speech can lead to things he wants and that he can have an impact on his environment. This is often taught by providing many learning opportunities so the child can experience success across many situations. Often, instructors set aside specific times or sessions to focus on building this skill, providing intense and repeated practice. Usually, there comes a time when the child demonstrates this skill readily. At that point, he may frequently ask for things across many environments. When that is the case, it becomes a problem if the instructor continues to set up a specific time for requesting. If the learner you are working with clearly has the ability to request things, then you should be asking yourself and the team, "Why are we doing mand *training*?" and, "What is being trained if he already has this skill?"

Possible Negative Effects of Formal Mand Training Beyond When It Is Needed

Honoring children's requests and continuing to reward their attempts to communicate are goals that should always be part of how we interact with them. However, creating a formal teaching session that is focused on requesting may be problematic if it persists after the child has already mastered manding. Some of the unintended negative effects may include:

Teaching "Request" vs. "No Request" Times. As experienced clinicians and consultants, the authors have all seen the following scenario: Learning sessions begin by having an instructor or therapist display an array of items to the child. These may be presented as options for "earning" (something the child will work for) or as enticing items that are meant to help the child view the work setting as a positive place. The child may enter this setting, sit down, ask for things, and get them—which is a positive way to begin a work session. However, sometimes we have seen a timeframe established, possibly arbitrarily, during which the child is expected to mand. For example, for ten minutes or so, the student is reminded to request things and then is given access to them, and this is repeated for the "mand" training portion of the lesson. Following a series of successful mands, the enticing items are cleared away so that the actual "work" can begin.

This creates a situation in which the time to request and access cool things is signaled by having the options displayed in front of the child, and then there is a change in the environment and all the items are swept away and the work begins. For some children, this will lead to the idea that requesting is limited only to those times when items are presented to them; in other words, they should only request when an array is available.

Unnatural or Less Natural Learning Environments or Situations. This very rich and rewarding context that we create during a mand session is incredibly important early in a child's learning history. We are trying to harness his motivation and help him learn the power of communication. However, there are very few environments or situations in life that are like a mand session—where you get what you want over and over just for asking.

One of our goals in teaching children with autism is to create very structured environments to bring about and sustain the behavior we'd like to build in them. Once we have taught important skills, we need to help children continue to be successful and to persist even outside of specialized and focused environments. This will help ensure that these skills we spend time teaching will translate to other environments and last over time after our teaching.

In order to do this, as teachers we need to consider what elements of the environment will be important to focus on to sustain the behavior we want to maintain. For requesting behavior, it is important to help children with ASD learn that the most important element in the environment is a listener. In other words, eventually, we would like them to have the skill to mand for something whenever a listener is available—someone to hear and grant their request. We do not want them to make requests only when arrays of enticing items are presented.

Creating Challenges for Motivation during Later Learning Activities. Sometimes shifting focus from basic to more advanced mand training during a teaching session sends the following message to a child with ASD: "Now you have to work really hard for all those things I just gave you." Remember, when initial mand training begins for a child with autism, the behavior of asking, in and of itself, is hard work. The child is not naturally making requests that are directed to a listener, so we have to create a teaching situation to help that occur and reward it when it does.

However, after successful mand training, a child has a lot of experience making basic requests. If we continue to reward those basic requests with really motivating items at the beginning of a work or teaching session, we will not be able to effectively use those same motivating items to reward success in doing the more difficult skills we are trying to teach. This is related to the concepts of *satiation* and *ratio strain* which were described in chapter 1. A child may get his fill of the good stuff that is always available for manding at the beginning of the session, and then won't be interested in working harder for those same items later in the work session.

What Can We Do about the Problem?

So how can we avoid the problems that can arise if we fail to change our teaching approach once a child has mastered basic manding? And what can we do if we see signs of potential problems? The sections below cover the most important steps to take.

Consider the Child's Full Learning History

What I mean by this is to think about whether the child has benefited from learning how to mand, and if so, under what conditions? Has he already succeeded in requesting preferred items in the current situation? This includes the current instructor or teacher, the current classroom or setting, and the current activity. Also, it is important to consider whether the child is willingly approaching the area where learning is going to take place, and whether he has had experience receiving and participating in enjoyable things while in that setting or situation.

If the answer is yes, it is likely that mand training should no longer be a primary focus. This may need to be revisited if there is a change, such as a new instructor, or new or harder work being presented. Or, you may need to go back to creating mand situations at the outset of a learning session if the child is being asked to leave a very fun activity to begin a less preferred work activity.

Avoid Programmatic Rules and Timeframes

Another important consideration is that instructors should *be cautious about establishing "mand time" or a rule about the number of minutes or the number of mands* that are scheduled into a teaching session. Often, teachers may set up certain rules about manding as a way to remind themselves and other instructors that communication is such a core skill and area of need for children with ASD that it should always be a focus of instruction. Having "manding" on the schedule ensures that it is not ignored. However, the focus on manding and communication needs to be carefully woven into other instruction and activities throughout a child's learning. Scheduling separate "mand time" does not help to integrate this skill meaningfully into other lessons and activities.

Many of the authors of this book have observed well-meaning instructors who focus very specifically on manding during scheduled periods of time, but then are less likely to plan for ways to focus on manding throughout other functional activities. In other words, an instructor might then "cross manding off the list" of things that need to be taught, rather than continually evaluate and think about the skill. We recommend that instructors learn to find places to insert manding opportunities during other activities. For example, you might have the child choose a color for drawing when you hold up a few options, or "forget" to give the student a straw with his unopened juice box so that he needs to request a straw.

Work on Cooperation and Compliance

Other important ways to help avoid possible problems are to focus *on rewarding naturally occurring cooperation* and *systematically build compliance.* Early models of teaching children with ASD focused on establishing compliance; in some cases, this compliance was created by ensuring that children could not avoid or escape an instructor's instruction or a work session. "Compliance training" was done in many ways. In hindsight, it may be easy to criticize these models of instruction as being overly negative, punishing, or controlling. However, it is important to balance this assessment by considering other views and practices at the time—a time when many educators were of the opinion that children with ASD could not be taught at all. Teaching compliance and having children learn to respond to instructors was transformative and instrumental in establishing the expectation that children with ASD could learn with intensive and structured teaching.

With the onset of mand training, teaching methods began to focus on the compliance that emerged as a result of children experiencing positive outcomes associated with their learning environments. In other words, children with ASD were now learning to approach teachers or work areas because they could access good things—rather than approaching the teacher or work because they had learned that there was no way to avoid it.

Therefore, children with ASD who have participated in mand training often comply when instructors ask them to come to the work setting or to begin a teaching session. This compliance is a result of their experience with an instructor or environment that has been associated with many good things. However, this compliance may not automatically transfer to new or different situations.

Instructors may not realize that they have come to rely on offering enticing items or activities as a way to initiate learning sessions. It is important for instructors to learn how to engage students in a learning interaction that does not begin with an enticement. Further, they need to teach their students the important and fundamental life skill of compliance and help them develop it over time. Naturally moving from pure pairing, to manding, to building compliance with instructions is a progression that should always be examined.

Building Momentum. Skilled clinicians and teachers often create appealing work situations that are rich with rewards by gradually and systematically building their students' momentum and success within work situations. One way to accomplish this is to present simple and natural instructions or opportunities for a child to engage with learning materials successfully and independently. Examples:

- Provide the student with praise and other work rewards when he brings an object to the table, such as a puzzle piece to fit into a puzzle that is already on the table.
- During transitions from a play activity to work, ask the student to drop his toy into a bin you hold in front of him—an action that may occur naturally and that is also establishing compliance and a context in which the instructor is paired with familiar and easy instructions.

There is a body of research and literature on a concept called *behavioral momentum* that can be applied to understand the underlying process that is going on in situations like this. Behavioral momentum as a conceptual idea was named and explored by a researcher named John Nevin and his colleagues in 1983. Then, in 1988, researcher and psychologist F. Charles Mace and his colleagues applied Nevin's concept of behavioral momentum to the treatment of noncompliance in children. They showed that first presenting a series of requests or instructions that are easy or preferred for a child to follow (high probability requests) makes it more likely the child will then comply with a direction he would typically be less likely to respond to (low probability request). Skilled pediatricians may naturally use this concept with patients who are reluctant to have their tonsils examined. The doctor might say, "Where's your toe?" then, "Give me five!" and, "Can you touch your head?" before sneaking in the request to "Say ahhhh."

A caution about behavioral momentum and the use of a "high probability request sequence": some research studies have shown this to be a powerful intervention when a child is displaying problem behavior. For example, to minimize problem behavior, or as a consequence to a behavior problem, a teacher or instructor may present a number of instructions to a child. All of the authors of this book have seen that this is sometimes done at an unnaturally high speed and may take on an unnatural quality. This rapid-fire delivery of instructions is not necessarily what was studied in the research, and we do not advocate this approach as a general practice. Addressing challenging behavior using behavioral momentum as a specific intervention within a comprehensive behavior plan is a separate topic and one that should be overseen by a behavior analyst or trained educator. We are really talking about starting at a place where a learner can be successful and building the work sessions from there.

Being Aware of Cues That Signal Time for Play or Work. It is also extremely important to be aware of other cues in the learning situation that might signal to the student 1) when lots of fun or preferred things are available, and 2) when "work" begins and these things are not available, or, at least, not "freely" available. The most obvious way instructors signal that transition from playtime to work time is to collect a student's preferred toys or treats in a reward bin, and have that out in the open to begin a work session. Too often, after some period of free or frequent access to these things, the instructor puts the bin away, or puts it on the floor, which signals a big change for the student.

In that example, the cue that work is beginning is very obvious. However, careful observation may indicate that there are other more subtle cues sometimes, in situations in which there aren't reward bins available. Sometimes, actions such as an instructor pulling out a clipboard or datasheet may be the signal that a change is about to happen in the work session.

It is not a problem, per se, if children learn to recognize the onset of work. However, when children are young or new to intervention, there should be less of a contrast between "work" and "play" or "leisure," since the first skills to be taught are skills that can and should be used everywhere—including during activities considered to be play or leisure or free time. In the case of a new learner, it should be difficult for an observer to notice a clear difference between work and play.

Noticing a difference between work and play or identifying the cues that signal the distinction is important if this difference or cue somehow affects the child's learning or behavior. For example, if the moment the instructor takes out the clipboard or asks Charlie to pull in his chair he begins to engage in problem behavior, the instructor needs to evaluate two things. One, the instructor should consider what might be the negative part of the work situation; for example, is the work too difficult? Is there sufficient motivation for Charlie? Secondly, the instructor should become aware of the cue to which Charlie is responding and see if the cue can be avoided or paired with other things. For example, perhaps the clipboard can be present even during play and other fun activities as well. Or, perhaps Charlie can be asked to pull in his seat at times other than work, maybe pulling his seat in for a treat or reward.

I can recall working with a boy whose team always preceded work sessions and demands with his name, but did not call his name at any other times. For this little guy, hearing his name set off tantrums until we started pairing his name with access to good things and refrained from using his name as part of every work demand.

As a child gains more experience with intervention, it is crucial to understand the cues that are meaningful to him, and to be aware of how he is interpreting the environment. If a child is responding to unintentional or subtle cues in the teaching session, the instructor may not be aware of this. Often, an instructor may not be able to identify these cues without asking someone who is new to the situation to observe a teaching session. Paying more attention to these cues can help an instructor introduce specific cues that are planned and can be developed into visual schedules or other supports that can be an important part of increasing a child's independence over time.

Summing Up

The goal of teaching children with ASD is to give them the skills they need to access rewarding activities in their lives. As they grow and learn, the skills become more complex, and the array of rewards and experiences expands. Our job as educators is to make sure that we are continuing to help our learners expand their skills, and doing so in a way that is systematic and allows them to be successful. Finding this balance in a teaching situation is something we have all seen. The bar needs to be set just right—we can't establish expectations that our student can't reach, but it is just as problematic to reward skills and behaviors at a level that doesn't encourage more learning. With this chapter as a guide, it is our hope that parents and teachers can recognize situations that might be occurring and develop strategies to address these concerns.

SELF-ASSESSMENT: Are You "Giving It Away?"

Here are some questions to ask to determine how "Don't Give It Away" might be a factor in a learning situation.

1. What consequence is being used to reinforce desired behavior?

   ■ What is the child supposed to do? What will happen when he does it? _____

   _____

   ■ Will that result make him more likely to do the same thing again in the future? _____

2. What behavior is the learner using to get access to the reinforcer?

   ■ Is the child doing what the instructor wants him to do to get the reward? _____

   ■ If not, what is the child doing instead? Why? _____

   _____

3. Is the student manding for the item/consequence?

   ■ Do you know if manding is in the learner's repertoire? How do you know this? _____

   _____

   ■ Is this clear from watching this session? _____

   ■ Is mand training needed? How do you know this? _____

   _____

   ■ Is there an opportunity for the learner to initiate the mand?

   _____

4. Is pairing part of this session?

   ■ If yes, what things are being paired together (intentionally)?

   _____

- Is it possible that "unintentional" pairing is occurring?

  _____

- If pairing is not part of this session, should it be?

  _____

5. How could you distinguish between lack of pairing and lack of motivation? (See pp. 4–5 for signs that a learner is not motivated.) _____

   - Do you observe the use of negative reinforcement? (i.e., Do what I ask, and then "Go play.") _____

     _____

6. Does the environment indicate whether "reinforcement" is available? _____

   - If so, how? _____

   - If not, in what way? _____

   - Should the environment indicate whether reinforcement is available? _____

7. Could satiation (see pp. 7–10) be a concern with this learner/these preferred items? _____

   _____

8. Could the instructor reward naturally occurring/high probability responses? _____

   - What might this look like? _____

     _____

Julia Clark is a six-year-old girl with a diagnosis of ASD. Since the age of three, Julia has been attending a school program that uses the principles of applied behavior analysis to teach young children on the autism spectrum.

Julia's mother, Mary, has noticed some improvement in her daughter's language, self-care, and play skills. She has been concerned, however, with the time it takes Julia to acquire new skills.

When Julia started her current program, the staff first conducted an assessment of her skills. Based on the results of this assessment, the team decided to focus on language, play, and self-care skills. Although Julia has made some progress in these areas, the staff, like Mary, have also reported concerns about the rate at which Julia acquires new skills. During sessions, Julia responds inconsistently when learning new skills. Even within the same program, sometimes she responds correctly and other times she does not. Because of this inconsistent responding, it seems to take Julia a long time to learn each targeted skill. Even after she learns a new response, Julia doesn't always get it right.

During a recent parent observation, Mary and Allison, the school's behavior analyst, watched Julia learning to receptively identify "things you can wear." After the teacher presented Julia with the instruction, she would sometimes respond correctly by touching the shirt, pants, or other item of clothing. Other times, Julia would look out the window or at her hand while the teacher was giving the instruction. When Julia wasn't looking at the teacher, she wouldn't respond. When Julia didn't respond, her teacher would physically prompt her to touch the correct item.

Julia has been earning tokens for correct responses during her teaching sessions. After earning five tokens, Julia exchanges the tokens to play with toys that she enjoys, such as puzzles, an iPad, and books. Mary had initially agreed that these were good practices and this system would be ideal to use to reinforce her daughter's correct responses. Now, as Mary observed Julia's inconsistent responses to the teacher's instructions, she remembered the behavior analyst's explanation of how reinforcement worked. When reinforcement is delivered immediately after a response, it increases or strengthens the response that just occurred. Because reinforcement works by increasing the behavior that just occurred, Mary wondered if Julia should be receiving tokens when she was turning away from the teacher or looking out the window. Was it OK to deliver the instruction or reinforcement when Julia wasn't even paying attention?

After the observation, Mary met with Allison and the team to review the observation. Allison explained that these other, off-task behaviors could be interfering with Julia's learning. When Julia was looking out the window or playing with her fingers, she was not attending to the teacher.

Allison pointed out that Julia was missing many prerequisite or "learning-to-learn" skills (Leaf & McEachin, 1999). For example, Julia wasn't consistently attending to the teacher when an instruction was presented. When working with materials on the table, Julia didn't look at or scan the materials. At times, when asked to touch or find an object, Julia would continue to look out the window or just reach out to touch one of the items without looking. If Julia responded correctly by chance, she was given a token. Delivering tokens at times when Julia wasn't attending could potentially be reinforcing off-task behavior. Julia's progress was being impeded by her lack of attention to the teacher and her failure to scan, as well as by the teacher's reinforcement of her off-task behavior.

Without these learning-to-learn skills, Julia's rate and quality of skill acquisition will be compromised. Allison also explained how important these skills will be to Julia in the future so that she can participate in small- and large-group activities. The team needed to back up and focus on building these important foundation skills.

Overview of the Issue: "Learning-to-Learn" Skills

Many basic learning skills play a role in increasing the success of any child. The prerequisite skills described in Julia's case are often referred to as "learning-to-learn" skills (Leaf & McEachin, 1999).

Without these skills, acquisition of new skills will be challenging and a slow process.

Leaf and McEachin (1999) describe "learning-to-learn" skills as an essential component of the beginning stage of a therapeutic program. These skills, which include attending, sitting appropriately, understanding that responding to instructions will result in rewards, and remaining on-task, are taught so that the child is "ready to learn." Watching a teaching session with a child who is ready to learn will reveal some clear indicators of what being "ready to learn" looks like. These skills include:

- attending to the instructor and materials,
- scanning or shifting attention from one stimulus to another,
- waiting quietly for instructions,
- waiting for feedback from the instructor after responding.

These are the skills needed to build the foundation for successful learning experiences (Leaf & McEachin, 1999). We need to take the time to ensure that the children we are teaching have these prerequisite skills before targeting other skills.

What Do Problems with Learning-to-Learn Skills Look Like?

We frequently hear that time is so precious for children with ASD. There is often pressure to move quickly and to start teaching academics, language, social, and self-care skills so that our students will catch up to their peers. Sometimes, in our haste, we forgo taking the time to teach the prerequisite, learning-to-learn skills that will increase the rate of acquisition and the learner's long-term success.

Many children with ASD have difficulty with attending, orienting, and shifting attention. Impairments in attending can affect educational progress and development of social skills. Teaching language, academic, and social skills before teaching the student how to attend can decrease the rate at which these skills are acquired.

Like Julia, many individuals with ASD have difficulties identifying stimuli to which they should attend in a learning situation. Often, multiple stimuli are present. For example, there are many different objects and people inside the classroom, as well as outside distractions such as trees blowing in the wind outside the window. With all of these distractions, it is difficult for the child to determine where to direct her attention. If the child isn't attending to the speaker or materials, she will acquire new skills slowly and the skills acquired may be of poor quality.

Many children with ASD begin learning in a format called discrete trial instruction. Discrete trial instruction structures the environment to help children with ASD to attend to the relevant objects and people in the environment while learning. Objects that are not relevant to the target skill and lesson are put away. With only the relevant objects and people present, such as the teacher and the instructional materials, the child has fewer opportunities to attend to irrelevant objects and materials. With the learning environment designed in this way, learning-to-learn skills can be the primary focus of a student's program.

Just as watching a child who is ready to learn can tell us a lot about important foundation skills, watching a child who is missing those skills will reveal some important differences. Sometimes, when we watch a teaching session with a child like Julia, we see an absence of attending. These behaviors include the following:

- reaching toward materials before the instruction is given,
- looking away from the teacher or the materials,
- turning away from the teacher before he or she provides corrective feedback or reinforcement,
- attending to only one or some of the materials presented, instead of scanning all of the materials, before responding.

Responses such as these are obstacles to acquiring new skills. These are signs that the child is not ready to learn. Think about how difficult it would be to learn something new if you weren't hearing the information the teacher was sharing. If the child isn't looking at the materials or teacher, she will most likely be guessing when responding to the instruction. To learn new skills, a child needs to look at and wait for the teacher to present an instruction. If a child is reaching toward the materials before she has been asked to do something, she is not attending to the teacher. A child also needs to attend to and listen to the teacher after responding in order to learn from feedback. This will make it more likely that the child will respond correctly next time. Learning new skills also involves shifting attention from one object to the next. Without this skill, the child will not be attending to all of the materials or individuals involved in the teaching session.

Where Does the Problem Come From?

When Julia started school, her team was so excited to get her started. All of the teachers were anxious to finish her assessment and to begin implementing her skill acquisition programs. In their haste to get started on teaching Julia new skills, the staff didn't teach her to attend to (look at) the teacher before an instruction was delivered or to wait for feedback after responding. Instead, they tried to establish eye contact by holding a preferred item near their eye before delivering the task demand. If that didn't work, they gave the instruction while Julia wasn't looking and prompted the correct response. They then recorded her response as "incorrect." Julia's data showed inconsistent responding over many sessions.

In the past, some programs that used the principles of applied behavior analysis taught students with ASD to attend to the speaker in the context of a discrete trial program. This involved asking or prompting the child to look at the speaker immediately before the adult delivered a task demand. Practicing "looking" and attending in this way was aversive for some learners because after they attended to the speaker, they were immediately presented with a demand. Some children would avoid eye contact because they learned that looking at the instructor wasn't followed by "good things." Instead it was followed by the presentation of a task demand.

Since some children with ASD avoided eye contact with teachers to delay task demands, it was thought that not attending was an avoidance response, a way for the child to get out of doing the work. Because of this, some practitioners proposed that if the child didn't attend to the teacher after the teacher said, "Look at me," the instruction should be delivered anyway. Instructors thought that by doing this, they would not be reinforcing the child's lack of attending by letting her avoid or delay work.

What Can We Do about the Problem?

Even with well-meaning intervention, it is not at all uncommon for these problems to arise. Signs that a student is missing learning skills can and should be addressed whenever they are noticed. Below are a number of specific steps to take to help make working on these fundamental skills a priority during instruction.

Target Eye Contact and Attending during Preferred Activities

One of the most basic principles of applied behavior analysis—which has been proven time and again—is that when a person's response is followed by preferred activities or items, that response is more likely to occur again. This is the definition of how *reinforcement* works, as we reviewed in chapter 1. When teaching children to attend to an instructor, we therefore want to be sure that eye contact is followed by access to a preferred item or activity so that eye contact will be likely to occur again.

Manding or requesting is a skill that is taught to the learner as a beginning skill in his or her program and is described in more detail in chapter 2, "Don't Give It Away." This skill provides the learner with the opportunity to ask for and receive access to objects and activities she likes. Opportunities to mand or request provide a perfect opportunity to target eye contact.

After the child has learned a response that enables her to request things she really likes, such as by pointing or making sounds, you can begin to work on eye contact during manding. If the child makes eye contact while she is indicating what she wants (manding), give her the item immediately. If she does not make eye contact when manding, pause before handing the item to her. When the child makes eye contact when you withhold the preferred item, give access to the item immediately.

Some instructors may have concern about withholding something that the child just "asked" for. While this is an understandable concern, this is a place where the research and science of ABA can help. By withholding the item or activity, you are placing the mand on extinction, a technical term in ABA referring to a procedure in which we stop reinforcing a specific response. Remember, the response that you are not reinforcing in this scenario is a mand or request that occurs *without* eye contact. A mand or request that occurs *with eye contact* should receive reinforcement—and lots of it!

One of the side effects of extinction is variability in responding. This means that the child will begin to engage in different responses to try to access the same reinforcing item or activity. In other words, if the mand does not "work" to get the item or activity, she will try to do other things. One of these responses may be looking at the person holding the item. This procedure has been shown to be effective with children who do not demonstrate challenging behavior when access to preferred items is delayed. If your child or student starts to show problematic behavior when preferred items are withheld while waiting for eye contact, consult a behavior analyst. He or she can suggest strategies to help minimize the possibility of behavior problems while also increasing eye contact with requesting.

Wait for It

Another way in which staff can teach attending is to "wait for it." Initially, this may involve engaging the child in a fun activity she really enjoys. For Julia, this involved having the teacher sing her favorite song. After a few lines of the song, the teacher would pause and look at Julia. As soon as Julia looked at her, the teacher would immediately begin singing the song again. "Waiting" for eye contact while engaging your child or student during a preferred activity gives the learner a great opportunity to practice and be reinforced for attending to the instructor.

"Waiting for it" can also be used to increase attending in the context of a work session. This involves identifying a highly preferred item and holding it where the child can see it but not reach it. As soon as the child is sitting quietly and looking at the teacher, the item is given to her.

After using Julia's favorite song to motivate her to make eye contact, Allison recommended that Julia's team improve her attending skills with the help of her favorite toys. When Julia is given a choice of several toys, she always chooses a puzzle or the iPad. Allison therefore recommended using the iPad and puzzles to teach Julia to attend. She explained that Julia would be motivated to look at her teachers when they had or were holding these items. To teach attending, the teacher would hold the iPad or put the puzzle in a place where Julia could see it. Initially, as soon as Julia looked at the teacher, the item was given to her.

In the beginning, Julia's instructors had to wait a few minutes for Julia to look at them, and they worried that they were wasting important time. Fortunately, the instructors had a long history with Julia of providing her with praise and positive things, and it wasn't too long before Julia began to look at the teacher within a shorter amount of time.

Then, as Julia consistently sat and looked at the teacher, some of her attending responses were immediately reinforced and others were not. That is, the teachers would, at times, give Julia a toy as soon as she looked at them and had "quiet" hands. Other times, the teacher would present a simple instruction as soon as Julia looked at him or her with quiet hands. As Julia's attending becomes more consistent, she will receive reinforcement for attending more and more infrequently. Eventually, Julia will only be reinforced after she responds correctly to the teacher's instruction.

Sometimes, as the title of this chapter indicates, an instructor has to wait for the child to attend. Often, there is pressure on an instructor to begin work immediately and give the child instructions right away. This is frequently why instructions may end up being given when a child isn't paying attention. It may seem obvious that a child is more likely to attend to a teacher when she is motivated by a reward that is available or when the teacher or situation has been adequately paired with reinforcement in the past. In these cases, the teacher may not need to wait too long!

All too often, however, the authors of this book have encountered instructors who have waited for children for a long time only to have them never spontaneously attend. In these cases, some instructors move quickly into prompting responses or having the child work even though she is not attending, rather than finding ways to make motivation and attending more likely. Many other chapters in this book address those problems (see chapters 2, 4, 6, and 8).

Wait for Feedback

Up until now, we have focused on attending to a teacher's instructions and the things that are important at the beginning of a lesson or a teaching session. During discrete trial instruction, the child's response is followed by feedback from the instructor. Feedback is delivered in the form of an error correction or reinforcement. The likelihood of the child responding correctly during the next learning opportunity depends on the feedback or reinforcement delivered during prior learning opportunities. If the learner is not attending while reinforcement or corrective feedback is delivered, it is not likely he or she will respond based on that feedback in the future.

In an effort to provide reinforcement quickly, teachers may sometimes inadvertently reinforce off-task behavior. For example, if the student turns away from the instructor after a correct response and then receives the preferred item, it is possible that the off-task behavior was reinforced. In addition, the connection between the target response and the reinforcer is weakened.

If your child or student engages in off-task behavior immediately after responding correctly, pause and refrain from reinforcing her response. Instead, re-present the task demand. If she makes a "clean" response, give her the reinforcement. Instructors may hesitate to follow this approach because they want to reinforce the correct response. They may not want to place another demand on the child without first acknowledging that she got the response right. Caution should be used in these situations because the instructor may be reinforcing the off-task behavior or teaching a "chain." This means that by receiving reinforcement for off-task behavior, the child may learn and continue to engage in the off-task behavior after the response.

To increase the extent to which the child attends during feedback, assess her motivation prior to giving her instructions. Initially, ensure that she can see the highly preferred reward. Present simple instructions—that is, tasks that the child already has in his or her repertoire—to practice this skill. Immediately after the child responds, hold up the item and wait for her to look before giving her the item. We start with skills the child already has in her repertoire so she will receive reinforcement (rather than corrective feedback) and acquire the skill of looking at the teacher before reinforcement (or corrective feedback) is delivered.

Teach Visual Tracking

After her observation, Allison suggested that the team assess Julia's visual tracking skills. To teach Julia to visually track, Allison used puzzle pieces and Polly Pocket dolls, some of Julia's favorite toys. She first held these toys and moved them around in different locations. She asked Julia to "look" at the doll in each location. Julia tracked each doll as Allison moved it around.

During the next part of the assessment, Allison asked Julia to "look" at items on the desk as she pointed to them. Julia did not scan all of the items on the desk. The team discussed the importance of targeting this skill. So many skills require that Julia scan items on the desk. If Julia didn't learn to shift her attention from one stimulus to another on the table, how could she shift her attention in a setting with many more distractions present?

When students with ASD begin learning outside of the discrete trial teaching format, they are more likely to encounter distractions or irrelevant stimuli. Not only does this require shifting their attention from one stimuli to another, but it also involves attending while other irrelevant stimuli are present.

Attending with Other Stimuli Present

A large part of Julia's time in school is spent learning new skills in a discrete trial teaching format. Allison and the staff began to discuss teaching Julia to learn to attend in the presence of other stimuli, such as her peers and other distractions in the environment. This will help Julia learn to block out the irrelevant stimuli and focus on the relevant ones.

During discrete trial teaching, the teacher is often seated directly in front of the child. This makes it more likely that the learner will focus on and attend to the teacher. To help Julia learn to attend to the teacher when other stimuli are present, the teacher can begin to increase her distance from her. At first, Julia can learn to demonstrate skills she has already acquired with the teacher positioned at a distance of three to five feet from her. This distance should be increased gradually as Julia learns to follow instructions in this context.

Once Julia can demonstrate old skills with the teacher at a distance, new skills should be taught using this setup. In addition to increasing the distance of the teacher from the child, the number of peers present should also be increased gradually.

To learn successfully in a group, students must be able to shift attention from one speaker to the next and from the speaker to books, whiteboards, or other materials referenced by the speaker. To help a learner with ASD learn to attend in a group, you can gradually increase the number of students included in the group and duration of the lesson. In addition, to teach the student to shift attention from the teacher to a peer, reinforce the student for attending to a peer. This skill can be shaped by asking the student with ASD questions about a peer's response or telling her to "copy" what a peer did or said. To correctly respond, the child must wait quietly, listen to the teacher, and pay attention to her peer. Depending on the child's skills, learning opportunities such as these should be provided to teach group attending skills.

Summing Up

Although we want to teach our children with ASD as much as we can and as quickly as we can, it is imperative that we take the time to teach attending skills. To be successful in their educational programs, children first need to learn the following skills:

- to look at the teacher and materials,
- to wait for the teacher to deliver the instruction,
- to look to the teacher for feedback after responding, and
- to shift their attention from one object or person to the next.

These skills can be taught in the context of preferred activities or while teaching the child to ask for things that she likes. If we take the time to teach these skills from the start, we will maximize the child's quality of instruction and rate of learning new skills.

SELF-ASSESSMENT: Do You Need to Work on Waiting for It?

Here are some questions to ask to determine how learning-to-learn skills might be a factor in a learning situation.

1. Does the student reach toward the materials before the teacher gives the instruction?

   _____

2. Does the student look away from the task materials?

   _____

3. Does the student look away from the teacher before the reinforcer is delivered?

   _____

4. Does the student turn away from the teacher before the reinforcer is delivered?

   _____

5. What objects or people is the student attending to in the environment?

   _____

   _____

6. Does the student make eye contact with the teacher during a small group activity?

   _____

7. Does the student make eye contact with peers during a small group activity?

   _____

8. Based on your answers to the questions above, what learning-to-learn skills does the student need to acquire first?

   _____

   _____

4 | Hands Off
Benjamin Thomas

Jimmy Petrucelli is fifteen years old and received discrete trial instruction for many years for basic "learning-to-learn skills" such as attending, imitation, matching, following directions, and asking for things he likes. Now Jimmy is learning how to do office tasks such as sorting and filing documents as part of his pre-vocational training. After a few months of the filing lessons, Jimmy is still "learning." That is, he rarely initiates the tasks on his own, and he makes mistakes regularly. During his lessons, staff teaches by telling him how to do the tasks correctly, and even offers him choices of leisure activities to motivate him to complete tasks (or at this point, just to try on his own). **Nothing** *seems to be working, however.*

Sarah, the school behaviorist, offers some insight by closely examining their teaching methods. "What would it take for him to be 100 percent successful?" she asks the staff. In the past, they report, Jimmy learned many skills when they used hand-over-hand guidance while teaching. Sarah suggests they try physical guidance again when teaching him the filing tasks. That is, when Jimmy is given an office document, staff should immediately use their hands to help him grasp the document and then place and release it into the appropriate file folder. This type of teaching should minimize his mistakes as well as ensure he understands what is expected of him. She calls this "errorless" teaching.

__Possible Ending #1:__ A week later, Sarah stops by Jimmy's classroom to observe his filing program in action. "You were right. Jimmy likes the physical guidance," a staff member informs her. "He grabs our hands right away to help him." Unfortunately, Jimmy hasn't made any progress in his filing skills without the help. Sarah notices Jimmy watching his friend on the computer across the room. Meanwhile, a staff member *physically guides him through the filing lesson. He isn't attending to the task at all! "This is a problem," Sarah thinks.*

Possible Ending #2: Two weeks later, Sarah returns to the classroom to check on Jimmy's progress. Expecting to see an "employee-of-the-month" worthy performance, she instead finds him sitting on the floor and refusing to transition to the filing station. Staff reports that sure enough, Jimmy was on-task and making few mistakes when they used physical guidance. In fact, he quickly initiated tasks and even hurried to finish them as soon as they reached for his hands. After a few days, however, he started whining and keeping his distance when it was time for his pre-vocational lessons. Now he just avoids being near staff altogether. Sarah wonders what could have gone wrong....

Overview of the Issue: Using Prompts in Teaching

In its most basic form, the process of teaching students with autism spectrum disorders follows the three-term contingency: Antecedent-Behavior-Consequence. The antecedent is an event, such as an instruction or some cue, in the environment that informs a learner "It's time to do or say something" (e.g., *behave* in a certain way). For example, telling a student to pull out his math workbook is an antecedent for starting a math lesson. Similarly, asking a child to state his home address is an antecedent for recalling specific personal information. While reinforcement increases correct responding, some learners may not have these correct response in their repertoires, or know when to display them. Therefore, teachers use prompts to help students respond correctly and acquire new skills.

What Are Prompts?

In general, a prompt is any form of assistance that helps a learner respond correctly in a given situation. Within the three-term contingency of teaching, some prompts can be used immediately after instructions or events (i.e., antecedents) to ensure the child responds correctly. For example, a teacher might say, "Show me the blue car" and then immediately guide the child's hand to the blue car as a prompt. Prompts may also be used as a corrective consequence following a learner's mistake or lack of response. Suppose the child responds to the instruction in the previous example by touching a red car (in error). As a corrective prompt, the teacher might state, "This is the blue car" while simultaneously pointing to the blue car or guiding the child's hand to the blue car.

Overall, prompts are used as extra help (i.e., supplemental stimuli) in a teaching situation to enhance skill acquisition by increasing the likelihood a learner engages in the correct behavior (Foxx, 1982). Once the individual begins to respond correctly with a prompt, the prompt should then be systematically lessened until he independently responds to naturally occurring antecedents in his environment. This is called "fading" a prompt. Fading is necessary to allow the learner to respond to naturally occurring situations and achieve the maximum amount of independence.

Choosing Prompt Strategies

This chapter aims to help parents and teachers select the most appropriate teaching prompts. Accordingly, there are many forms of prompting that can be used, and many of these will be discussed. Some involve direct assistance from another person like verbal instructions or hand-over-hand guidance (MacDuff, Krantz & McClannahan, 1993). Other prompts include adaptations to the physical environment such as using pictures or text to enhance verbal directions (Krantz & McClannahan, 1993), or color-coding materials for a task (e.g., Dube, McDonald, McIlvane & Mackay, 1991) to increase the likelihood that the correct item will be selected. Allowing more time for a person to respond is also considered a type of prompt (e.g., Charlop, Schreibman & Thibodeau, 1985).

Choosing appropriate prompts for teaching can depend on a number of factors related to the skill being taught, as well as characteristics of the learner. Although this book cannot give a complete review of all prompts and their uses, experienced teachers and behavior analysts should have a grasp on these concepts. Readers are encouraged to refer to sources such as the following for a more complete discussion:

- the chapter on behavior analytic teaching procedures by Ahearn, MacDonald, Graff, and Dube (Sturmey & Fitzer, 2007; pp. 56–64),
- *Behavior Modification in Applied Settings,* 7th edition (Kazdin, 2013; pp. 42–45), or

■ *Applied Behavior Analysis,* 2nd edition (Cooper, Heron & Heward, 2007; pp. 401–409)

Many instructors rely on physical guidance as a "go to" prompt. Physical guidance is especially common during the initial stages of discrete trial teaching when children need to acquire new skills, and is often used as a corrective prompt when a learner makes a lot of mistakes. While using your hands to guide a student to respond correctly is almost a surefire way of ensuring success in a lesson, physical prompts are not always the most appropriate for some learners or tasks. Physical guidance also may not always prepare an individual to respond to natural situations in his environment without careful planning. That is, students may come to rely on physical guidance to respond correctly, rather than responding to other cues, instructions, or situations in the environment.

Choosing appropriate prompting strategies can lead to positive results and skill acquisition for many individuals with ASD, while lack of attention to this aspect of teaching can develop into problems like those described earlier in Jimmy's lessons. This chapter will focus on diagnosing instructional problems related to the use of physical guidance and offer solutions for remediating these problems to promote successful learning.

The Role of Physical Guidance in Teaching

Physical guidance is a type of prompting that has many names, including graduated guidance, manual prompts, hand-over-hand prompts, or simply physical prompts. Physical guidance is any type of assistance that involves physical contact between the instructor and the learner, to help that learner respond correctly or appropriately.

Physical guidance is often useful for teaching physical skills such as motor imitation to very young children. Often, imitation is one of the first steps in teaching children to pay attention to others. Being able to imitate others is considered a critical social learning skill (Ingersoll, 2008). That is, once a child can attend to others and then learn new skills by copying other people, many new skills will begin to emerge naturally or on command through observational learning. Physical guidance is appropriate in these situations, as very young children with developmental disabilities may not imitate others naturally.

Physical guidance may also be appropriate for older children who are learning more advanced motor skills. Some skills involving movements and actions may be taught more effectively with physical guidance than with verbal instructions or models. For example, imagine teaching a child how to tie his shoe using only verbal instructions. In that example, it is clear why helping a child actually position and move his hands as necessary is more effective. Additionally, when someone is learning skills in which safety is paramount, such as properly holding a newborn sibling or using tools and knives, the skill may be taught best with some level of physical guidance.

Other than for the situations described above where physical prompting may be needed, it is generally preferable to move on to other forms of prompting. For example, the goal in teaching children to imitate others and respond to models is to reduce the need for using physical guidance to teach other skills in the future. Therefore, instruction that continues to rely on physical guidance for learners who have skills beyond basic "learning-to-learn" skills (such as imitation) may indicate problems in teaching interactions. The next section offers guidance for diagnosing potential problems related to physical guidance in a variety of teaching situations.

What Do Problems with Physical Guidance Look Like?

When hand-over-hand guidance is used in the following situations, it is often a sign that something else is a problem in the teaching situation. The situations include using physical prompting with:

- a student who is not oriented to or attending to a task,
- a student who is not motivated to respond or is noncompliant, or
- a student who has previously demonstrated the ability to perform the task independently (without hand-over-hand guidance).

As noted earlier, physical guidance is useful in helping children acquire new skills. But, teachers may also use physical guidance to help students pay attention during lessons. This is a problem. Task materials and other related items such as a table, chair, and perhaps the teacher should become cues for attending. By attending, we generally mean that the child's head and body are facing the task area, and that he is not displaying interfering behaviors (e.g., Sarakoff & Sturmey, 2004). Teachers should always avoid using their hands to physically guide a student's head to teach him to attend.

Using physical guidance to prompt attending might indicate that the student is not motivated to participate in the task, rather than that he does not know how to attend. This problem is easily identified if the student has previously shown appropriate attending behavior.

Similarly, if you need to use physical guidance to help a student during a previously acquired skill, it can suggest a problem in motivation or discrimination rather than an attending skill deficit. For example, once a child has learned to touch and point, it should no longer be necessary to use physical guidance to help him form these hand gestures. The problem here may lie in the teaching materials, such as overly complex pictures on a flashcard. Noncompliant or avoidance behaviors during "known" tasks are usually quite salient indicators of problems with the child's motivation. If he knows how to respond correctly but doesn't do so, this might be more of a "won't do" vs. "can't do" issue. Therefore, using physical guidance for teaching would be contraindicated in these situations.

Where Does This Problem Come From?

It is not a surprise that physical prompts are used in a number of these situations, and that many instructors continue to resort to this prompting strategy. Some of the most common reasons for this include the following scenarios:

"Working Through" Noncompliance. Instructors often use physical guidance to redirect a student's noncompliance as a strategy to "work through" problem behaviors the person uses to escape nonpreferred situations. In the context of a behavior support plan, preventing escape from demands (following problem behavior) is a procedure called "extinction." Extinction reduces problem behavior by preventing the person from getting access to a reinforcing consequence that maintains the behavior. For example, when Joe has a tantrum because he doesn't want to complete math worksheets, his problem behavior helps him temporarily avoid the task. To work through his noncompliance, Joe's instructors may use physical guidance to prevent him from

using tantrums to escape the work. In this sense, physical guidance is used to teach the learner that engaging in problem behavior is *not* the correct response and will no longer result in escaping the situation. For Joe, the appropriate behavior should be asking for a brief break. The message that may be conveyed (indirectly) by an instructor in such a situation is "You can do it yourself, or I can help you." In other words, the instructor is communicating that there is an expectation for the student to do something (e.g., the math worksheet) and the student has an opportunity to do it independently, and if he doesn't, he will be physically prompted to do the task. *In this context, the physical guidance is not actually teaching new skills related to learning how to do the math worksheet, and is not meant to do so.* Physical prompting in this context is a behavior plan, addressing compliance, not a "teaching" strategy for improving math skills. It is important to recognize the significant difference in this type of situation where prompting is used for compliance compared to a scenario in which prompting is used for teaching a new skill. For example, if an instructor is physically guiding a student who is learning how to operate a vacuum, the physical guidance is teaching the student how to operate the vacuum, not preventing escape from the task.

As you can see, the problem of using physical prompting to *work through* noncompliance may stem from the instructor's confusion about the purpose of physical guidance in these situations. Teachers should remember that sometimes it is used as a teaching tool, and at other times a behavior management strategy. Thus, in teaching situations, teachers should be clear about the student's goals, thinking about his skill level and what kind of performance can be expected of him. Teachers should take caution not to interpret minor reluctance or mistakes as attempts to escape tasks (by using physical guidance to prevent this), as these may be signs of a slower pace of learning, lack of motivation, or the student not understanding task expectations. Conversely, teachers should also be wary about these signs as being truly motivated by task avoidance. In situations where it is not immediately clear (i.e., a learning challenge versus problem behavior), teachers are encouraged to use the experimental analysis techniques described later in this chapter.

Addressing Insufficient Motivation. Teachers may also feel at a loss when students are not motivated to participate in tasks. We know that physically helping a learner complete a task with hand-over-hand guidance will generally be successful. In essence, however, physical guidance is just slightly less support than offering the option of "hey, let me do that for you." If teachers have the mindset that there are only two choices—"help" versus "no help"—they run the risk of relying on physical guidance to urge their students to complete tasks that are taking too long. Teachers in these circumstances may not explore other prompt strategies, or other ways of increasing motivation, that may be more appropriate for promoting learning and independence.

Inconsistent Attending Skills. Some students do not consistently respond to the presence of a teacher or task materials without the use of a physical prompt to orient them. In this case, a student may not have established strong enough attending skills (see chapter 3). When this happens, an instructor may be very focused on the lesson at hand, and take it for granted that attending is a weakness for that student. The teacher may therefore overlook the fact that he or she is inserting physical guidance or contact into the task. In this situation, rather than back up and focus on building stronger attending skills, instructors continue to use physical support as a "work around."

"No Other Prompts Work." Along the same lines, if teachers are not aware of various other prompting strategies, they may not choose the appropriate method for a given task and may thus rely unnecessarily on physical guidance. "No other prompts work; we've tried everything" are phrases we've all heard on one or more occasions.

The problem here could be rooted in adherence to traditionally known prompts in the *least-to-most prompt hierarchy* (Miltenberger, 2011), or *three-step prompting* (e.g., Iwata, Dorsey, Slifer, Bauman & Richman, 1982/1994; Tarbox, Wallace, Penrod & Tarbox, 2007). For example, many texts describe giving instructions as the least intrusive form of prompting to be used as a first step in teaching (i.e., TELL prompt). Next, the level of assistance may be increased through modeling or gesturing, if necessary (i.e., SHOW prompt). Finally, helping the learner complete a task with physical guidance (i.e., DO prompt) is viewed as the most intrusive, but also the prompt most likely to be successful in most situations. Thus, physical guidance appears to be at the end of the line, or the *last resort* in prompting strategies. But there are many more approaches for offering and fading assistance. Table 1 (at the end of the chapter) presents a glossary of various alternatives to traditional prompting strategies that when used and then appropriately reduced can readily promote independent and correct responding.

Why Is This a Problem?

We discussed earlier how using physical guidance could assure a correct response from the student in many situations because the teacher is actually doing most of the work. Along these lines, physical guidance has the potential of informing learners that 1) they can relax their effort for a period of time and 2) on-task behavior is not necessary. In a nutshell, why lose energy if you don't need to? The student's expectations for instruction, in this instance, might become either tolerating physical contact or just taking a break from other activities. Meanwhile, *learning new skills* is not in the equation. In addition, the student's motivation for complying with tasks may be diminished, while the opportunity for engaging in other behaviors such as stereotypy or watching peers may be increased. We saw this happen when Jimmy watched a peer on the computer rather than learning his filing task in the first possible ending for the vignette at the beginning of this chapter.

Ensuring students with ASD are motivated to learn is essential to effective teaching interactions. A teacher who depends on using physical guidance, however, may ignore means of capturing or contriving a student's motivation. Our ultimate goals are for children to demonstrate desirable behaviors and in turn have a reason to do so in instructional settings and in the future.

On the other hand, some children with ASD may dislike receiving physical guidance. In this case, they may work hard and acquire skills to *avoid* physical guidance as corrective prompts. That is, their mistakes may inadvertently be punished when a teacher uses physical contact to correct them, and their correct responses are therefore reinforced by the absence of aversive physical guidance. Surely this is not a contingency we want to establish in our positive learning environments. By this token, creating negative learning environments with high probabilities of aversive consequences often leads to students using behavior problems to avoid or escape learning contexts. For example, we observed that Jimmy used problem behavior to avoid physical guidance during his lessons in the second possible ending to the vignette above.

Physical guidance may also be unnatural looking and even stigmatizing for older learners in many contexts. For example, if a job coach in a department store uses physical guidance with an adult client, it may look unusual to bystanders and may reduce the client's dignity.

Similarly, if a child with ASD receives physical guidance during a fifth-grade soccer game at recess, it will likely make him look "different" than his soccer-playing peers.

Reasons Why Relying on Physical Prompts Can Be a Problem

- Many students with ASD are passive recipients of physical prompting and may not learn from them.

- Reliance on physical prompting may reduce our likelihood of exploring different ways to motivate the individual.

- Caution: are we using punishment (i.e., a consequence that a learner will seek to avoid)? If physical prompts are used often with someone who dislikes the prompts, his responses may improve because he is trying to avoid physical contact. This means the learning environment has become aversive to him.

- Physical prompting might produce short-term effects (i.e., compliance) rather than long-term results (i.e., acquisition).

- Physical prompting can lead to behavior problems.

- Children get bigger; it will become harder and harder to physically redirect them as they age.

- Physical prompting looks unnatural in most community settings.

What Can We Do about the Problem?

The scenarios described in this chapter are common problems that we have seen in all kinds of learning situations. These situations can arise with all types of learners, in a variety of settings, and with many different instructors and circumstances. Almost universally, the resulting problems are the result of well-meaning instruction or teaching, and a desire to help the student be successful. When teachers are able to step back and critically examine a situation to recognize how it might have come to be, it can set the stage so they can address the underlying problems and plan for the next steps of instruction.

Stop and Think before Physically Prompting. The first step to diagnosing instructional problems related to prompting is to carefully consider the goals we hope to accomplish for the learner. In this situation, do we want him to acquire new skills? Or, are we focusing solely on compliance? If we are teaching new skills, then we should think about the most appropriate prompt for instructional context (i.e., task, skill, and setting). Remember, the goal is for the student to attend to the materials or task as a cue for responding correctly. Table 2 presents a sample list of skill programs with corresponding prompts that could be used as alternatives to physical guidance.

Consider the Learner's Motivation for the Tasks. Has the student demonstrated he has the skills required for the task, such as pointing, or has he previously shown mastery of the task? If yes, then the task may be too easy or boring for him and motivation may be a contributing factor.

Do you have an effective reinforcement system in place to encourage the child's attempts at completing the task at hand? If not, then a preference assessment must be conducted before teaching to determine items and activities that will motivate him to work hard (see chapter 1). Once we are sure the child will be motivated, and we have identified some appropriate prompting strategies for the skill to be taught, we must stop and think again about the child's preferences. Recall that all children have preferences for items and activities used as motivators for tasks. Similarly, they may also have preferences for types of prompts, and some prompts just may be more effective than others for particular children. Therefore, in the last step, it is time to *test prompting strategies.*

Test Prompting Strategies. A simple, experimental approach for testing the effectiveness of prompts is to select two similar skills, and teach each of them with a different prompt. For example, you might try teaching the child to read *twenty-one* with a vocal model, and to read *twenty-two* by superimposing the number 22 over the text. Comparing the number of trials it takes the child to learn to read the word with each teaching prompt may provide insight as to which is most appropriate. Similarly, you can select the same type of prompt for two skills (e.g., vocal model) but prompt one immediately, and prompt the other only after the child gives an incorrect response to determine if the errorless, or corrective, format is most effective for that student.

As noted earlier, testing in this manner may also allow teachers to analyze the relative ease or difficulty that different prompts afford a task. For example, ineffective prompts may contribute to task difficulty and escape motivated problem behavior, whereas effective prompts may decrease task difficulty and result in greater compliance.

Lastly, determining if students are dependent on prompts can also be examined through experimental comparisons. In errorless teaching, staff initially use more intrusive means of prompting to ensure success, and then reduce their assistance across opportunities to promote independence. When fading prompts in this manner, some students may get "stuck" at a certain level of dependence, however, and fail to gain independence. We saw evidence of Jimmy relying on staff assistance in scenario #1. It's important to remember that prompts might become the only reliable cue to respond (as part of the antecedent), as well as the only way students might engage in the correct behaviors, if not properly faded. Similar to comparing the effectiveness of two or more different prompts, teachers can also arrange probes in which the prompt is periodically absent, or time-delayed (e.g., Charlop et al., 1985) to analyze whether prompts are both effective, and if students are dependent on them. The logic follows that if a student is motivated by the consequence for correct responding, lack of assistance will result in delayed access to it. In these cases, the student should anticipate a response is necessary after the teacher's instruction, and then attempt to respond on his own (i.e., spontaneously or independently).

When making these comparisons, it's important to make sure other variables are similar, such as time of day, motivation, and even text font, for example. In this manner, you can be more certain about the effects of the prompting strategies.

Recap:
- Never prompt a basic response that is in the student's repertoire, such as touching or pointing to target stimuli. Remember: if a child knows *how* to point to something but is responding incorrectly, he just may not know *what* to point to, or he may not be motivated.
- *Teach/consider* responding to other prompts that are appropriate for the context.

Summing Up

In the end, it is important to remember that using physical guidance is an effective component of teaching children with ASD. However, if not used judiciously, the overuse of physical guidance can cause other learning or behavior problems. Using a prompt assessment in situations in which you are considering using a physical prompt can help you avoid the development of some of these problems and also pinpoint the priorities for teaching. The components of a prompt assessment described in this chapter include:

1. Consider the goals for instruction. For example, are you teaching a skill or trying to build compliance?
2. Use a teaching checklist (e.g., self-assessment at the end of this chapter) to observe existing programs for problems and note areas of success with other skills or prompts. Also consider the student's learning and prompting history and preferences.
3. Assess your student's preference and motivation for consequences, tasks, and materials.
4. Examine the task stimuli and discrimination expectations.
5. Arrange a specific comparison to compare prompts within a skill or similar programs once the learner's motivation is established. (See chapter 7 on individualization for examples of how to organize such comparisons.)

Remember, our goal is to help students learn to respond correctly, in the present and in the future. Using physical guidance to achieve an immediate correct response or behavior may not be effective in establishing long-term independent behavior. Stepping back from the teaching interaction and thinking about what you are trying to achieve will help ensure you are doing all you can to promote meaningful learning and your student's future success.

SELF-ASSESSMENT: Do You Need to Work on Being More "Hands Off"?

Here are some questions to ask to determine how the use of physical prompting might be a factor in a learning situation.

Observe teaching interactions within the classroom and respond to the following questions.

1. Is physical guidance being used?

   _____

2. Do any of the following situations apply to this teaching interaction:

   ☐ The student is not oriented/attending to the task.

   ☐ The student has previously demonstrated the task independently.

   ☐ The student is not motivated to respond.

   ☐ The student is noncompliant.

3. Do you see examples of "working through" noncompliance?

   _____

4. Has motivation been assessed or established?

   _____

5. Are physical prompts being used to:

   ☐ Orient the learner to the relevant stimulus?

   ☐ Orient the learner to the learning situation?

   ☐ Orient the learner to the instructor?

6. What other prompts (if any) could be used for that purpose?

   _____

   _____

7. How does the learner react to physical prompts?

_____

_____

8. What is the learner learning from the use of physical prompts?

_____

_____

9. What is the instructor learning from the use of physical prompts?

_____

_____

_____

10. What is accomplished with the use of physical prompts?

_____

_____

11. In this situation, is the student unable to perform the action or is the action not under stimulus control?

_____

_____

12. Describe the elements required for successful performance of the skill (for the skill to be under stimulus control). Will these be accomplished through physical prompting?

_____

_____

Table 1. Prompting and Fading Glossary

PROMPTING AND FADING

PHYSICAL GUIDANCE: The instructor uses physical contact such as hand-over-hand guidance; fade by reducing assistance or fading proximity of physical contact away from hands to hand over elbow, bicep, shoulder; light touch.

MODELING: Demonstrate the entire correct response; fade by modeling less of the response. Can be used for physical or verbal responses and used either in vivo or with video recordings.

GESTURES: Pointing to correct response, reaching to physically prompt, nodding head/looking/leaning in direction of correct response, expectant look or facial expression. Fading is usually done with a time delay.

VERBAL INSTRUCTIONS: Tell learner complete directions for completing a task; fade by reducing number of instructions or words, or giving indirect hints (e.g., ask questions about what he or she might need to do, give other examples, etc.).

STIMULUS PROMPTS: Changes in the learning materials to orient children toward materials or to facilitate a correct response. Below are types of changes that might be made:

Change Target Stimulus:
> **Position:** Move target item closer to student; fade by moving away/toward original position. For example, if teaching a child to identify a "book" in an array of 3 items on the table, placing the book much closer to the student, relative to the other items, may help him choose correctly because it is easier to reach or "stands out" in the crowd.

> **Size:** Increase the size of the target item to make it more noticeable than other choices; fade by decreasing size back to normal.

Color: Change the color of the target item compared to other choices; fade by adjusting hue to match that of other choices. For example, this may involve putting a red border around a target picture, and then removing the color over time.

Shape: Use a different shaped item (e.g., a triangle-shaped picture vs. square).

Intensity: Increase the sound or brightness of target stimulus. For example, when teaching a child to answer a question, the instructor may give the instruction in a normal volume and then say the answer more loudly to help the student pay attention to the answer instead of repeating the whole phrase.

Add an Extra Stimulus:
Auditory: Use audible sounds or recorded directions to facilitate a response. This may involve using a bell or timer to indicate it's time to change tasks or use the restroom.

Proximity/Shadowing: Remain near the student and then increase distance as the student becomes more independent. For example, walking behind a student as he transitions through the hallway, and then watching him from the classroom doorway as he demonstrates independence.

Olfactory: Use a preferred odor to guide a learner to attend, move, or change locations. For example, using preferred smells (e.g., cookies, pizza) to prompt an infant to roll over or lift his head.

Superimposition: Place a learned image or item over, behind, or within the target item/image (e.g., embedding the target reading word *one* within or over a picture of the numeral *1*) and fade out the learned image as the learner successfully responds.

Tactile prompt: Use a three-dimensional stimulus or sensory condition to facilitate a response. Examples include using various textures, a raised glue border to guide a student's pencil while tracing, or a vibrating timer in a child's pocket.

Time/Delay: Present instructions following a schedule (e.g., toileting every 20 minutes), or wait a specified number of seconds before prompting (e.g., 3–4 seconds) to allow for independent responses to occur.

Visual supports: Use pictures, writing, or type to facilitate a response. Examples include using a preferred item to direct child's attention toward correct response; reading sentence strips for help in conversation; photographs, drawings, pictures, sight words, lists of steps/checklists (i.e., visual instructions).

INDEPENDENT: Allow time for independent responses; use error correction prompts only in trials or opportunities after incorrect responses.

Table 2. Matching Prompts to Skill Acquisition Program

MATCHING PROMPT TO SKILL

FINE MOTOR
1. Model action
2. Stimulus: tactile, size
3. Time delay
4. Physical guidance

RECEPTIVE DIRECTIONS
1. Model
2. Stimulus: visual, positional
3. Time delay
4. Physical guidance

RECEPTIVE DISCRIMINATION (IDENTIFICATION)
1. Stimulus: change position, size, color, shape, or intensity of item; superimposition
2. Gesture
3. Time delay
4. Physical guidance

IMITATION (MOTOR, OBJECT)
1. Physical
2. Time Delay

MATCHING/SORTING
1. Stimulus: Change position, size, color, shape, intensity of item(s)
2. Gesture
3. Model

BLOCK DESIGN/PUZZLES
1. Stimulus: Change position, size, color, shape, intensity of item
2. Gesture
3. Model

ECHOIC
1. Model correct response

MAND/TACT
1. Model (echoic and fade)
2. Time delay

INTRAVERBAL
1. Vocal model
2. Visual stimulus: use acquired tact item, picture, word as prompt for intraverbal
3. Time delay

ACTIVITY SCHEDULES
1. Position/Proximity of tasks (e.g., ordering material left to right; near learner)
2. Visual stimuli to orient learner to tasks (e.g., color coding)
3. Proximity/Shadow
4. Physical

LEISURE SKILLS/PLAY SKILLS
1. Model
2. Stimulus: visual, positional
3. Physical

DAILY LIVING SKILLS
Toileting
1. Time: bring student to restroom following a schedule
2. Visual/textual: steps for task completion (use toilet, wash/dry hands), and mands
3. Tactile: vibrating timer (in conjunction with time schedule)
4. Auditory: audible alarm (in conjunction with time schedule)
5. Vocal model for restroom mands

Feeding
1. Physical (hand over hand for utensil use)
2. Model
3. Other procedures may be necessary for food selectivity or refusal

Routines/Jobs/Chores
1. Visual/textual prompts: to engage in task/routine or for each step of task
2. Positional
3. Tactile: vibrating timer to engage in task/routine
4. Auditory: audible alarm to engage in task/routine

SOCIAL SKILLS (INTERACTING WITH OTHERS)
1. Visual: use preferred items to direct students to approach others.
2. Visual/textual: use written sentence strips to prompt conversation.
3. Visual/picture: use pictures to cue student to engage in social interaction.
4. Model: model appropriate interaction.
5. Gesture: point/nod in direction of other people to cue interaction.
6. Positional: position student closer to target interaction partner (i.e., seat next to peers).
7. Proximity/shadow.

5 | Talk Less

Kate Fiske

Jacob was recently hired as a special education teacher in a local school district. The students in the classroom are six- and seven-year-olds who are minimally verbal and communicate with picture exchange communication systems and electronic devices. Jacob worked in the field for a few years as a teacher's assistant in another school before he got this job, and so he feels comfortable jumping in with these new students and modeling his teaching skills for the teacher's assistants.

Jacob learned in his old school district that, to increase language skills in learners with autism, it is important to fill their environment with language. Jacob takes this to heart and rarely stops talking when he is working with his students. His work sessions with students, in particular, are filled with language that is unrelated to the task at hand. For example, Jacob does not call his students by name and instead refers to them as "buddy" or "my man," provides lengthy justification for appropriate behavior ("You need to make sure that you are safe when you are sitting in your chair, so put all the legs back on the floor"), adds language to tasks to create a functional context for the activity ("I have a cat at home and he is so cuddly. I really love cats. Touch the picture of the cat"), and talks throughout the student's reinforcement breaks up until the moment he gives the next instruction ("You did such an awesome job with that; I am just so impressed with you. Way to go. Find the picture of the dog"). He is confident that he is providing his students with plenty of language models to build up their language skills.

However, when Claire, the school district behavior analyst pops into the classroom to observe some of Jacob's sessions, she is a bit surprised at what she hears. The language level that Jacob is using seems way be-

yond the students' comprehension, and she is unsure that they are able to understand the tasks and focus on the relevant information because Jacob has added so much language to his session. Claire knows that Jacob really wants to do the right thing for his students, but she wonders if the advanced level of language he is using may actually be doing more harm than good.

Overview of the Issue: Language Instruction

One of the primary symptoms of an autism spectrum diagnosis is a delay in social communication skills. The degree of difficulty that a student has in communicating with others varies considerably from learner to learner. Some children with autism have a clear grasp of *phonological* and *syntactic* use of language; that is, they understand how to produce the sounds necessary to speak words, and can string words together to create grammatically correct phrases, but they may struggle in areas of *semantics* and *pragmatics*. Semantics refers to an individual's ability to comprehend the meaning of words and phrases, while pragmatics refers to the effective use of language in social situations. For example, although a child may adeptly talk about a favorite topic, she may have difficulty maintaining conversations with peers her own age if the subject is not of interest. She may also have difficulty recognizing or understanding sarcasm in social situations.

For other children, however, acquisition of phonological and syntactic language proves incredibly challenging and makes the development of vocal language nearly impossible. Some research indicates that 25 percent of people with autism never acquire vocal language. Many of these individuals may come to rely instead on alternative forms of communication such as picture exchange systems, electronic augmentative communication devices, or sign language. Regardless of the mode of communication, language acquisition is often an intensive process that requires careful, systematic instruction.

Language instruction for learners with autism focuses on teaching both *expressive* and *receptive* language skills. Expressive language refers to the words one communicates to others, through spoken language, sign language, picture exchange, or other means. Expressive language can include the ability to repeat what other people say (known as *echoics*); talk about and label items, people, and activities in the environment (often referred to as *tacting*); ask questions of others (also known as *manding*); and respond to the conversational language of others (*intraverbals*). In addition to expressive language skills, teachers also focus on teaching receptive language. Receptive language skills center on an individual's ability to respond to and act on the language of another person, such as following directions to complete a specific task or identifying an item in the environment when someone states the name of the item or describes the item verbally.

Receptive and expressive language skills emerge separately and must both be taught as separate skills when considering the language needs of students with autism.

Maximizing Language Instruction

Anyone who has watched a neurotypical child develop has likely marveled at how easily his or her language skills emerge. With seemingly little instruction, many children learn two hundred or more words by their second birthday. In contrast, many children on the autism spectrum need instructors and parents to provide intensive instruction in developing receptive and expressive vocabulary and learning how to put words to use in various social settings.

Given the enormous task of teaching so many elements of language to children with autism, clinicians and researchers in the field have published curricula to help teachers systematically assess and teach the necessary skills. Perhaps the most well-known curricula is *Teaching Language to Individuals with Autism and Other Developmental Disabilities,* published by Mark Sundberg and James Partington in 1998. This book leads instructors through the assessment of language deficits, considering all functions of language discussed earlier—mands, tacts, and intraverbals—as well as *echoics*. The authors also offer specific strategies for teaching each component of social language. This manual is frequently paired with the *Assessment of Basic Language and Learning Skills-Revised*, by James Partington, which guides teachers through a systematic approach to assessment of social language skills.

As part of systematic skill instruction, Sundberg and Partington recommend that teachers and parents create a "language-based environment" for the learner, and describe this environment as a key component in encouraging language development for children on the spectrum. The authors point out that language training should be incorporated into all activities, and teachers should optimize opportunities students have to use language. For example, a teacher might capitalize on leisure time by playing a board game with a student but leave important playing pieces in the box so that the student must ask for them (manding), and may prompt the student to label the number of dots that appear on the dice (tacting), and ask her to answer questions about how she is enjoying the game (intraverbals). The teacher would praise and provide the student with other reinforcement for appropriate responses, and would be sure to provide the requested playing pieces when the student mands appropriately.

Another group of authors, Catherine Maurice, Gina Green, and Stephen Luce, emphasizes similar approaches to encourage language skills in *Behavioral Intervention for Young Children with Autism*. They specifically note that caregivers should "comment" on the environment around the child regularly to help increase her vocabulary. For instance, while a child is painting, the teacher can comment on items and activities in the environment such as "paint," "paintbrush," "blue," and "painting." Commenting provides effective models to the learner with autism for language that she can use in the future. Further, the authors suggest using exaggerated gestures, facial expressions, intonation, volume, and rate of speech to both model appropriate verbal and nonverbal language skills and also to keep work sessions interesting and varied. These approaches, and those described by Sundberg and Partington, maximize the amount of language that a student is exposed to throughout the day to help encourage language development. However, there are important differences between the methods for using language in teaching, as described by these authors, and the way in which Jacob was saturating the teaching environment with language. More on this later in the chapter.

In addition to incorporating language into naturally occurring activities, teachers are often encouraged to maximize the amount of instruction by providing frequent discrete trial opportunities for language learning (see chapter 6). In some programs that focus heavily on language-based instructions, instructors use specific practices to minimize downtime and maximize exposure to language and instruction. For instance, programs may attempt to maximize the number of trials in a session by de-emphasizing the *inter-trial intervals*. In discrete trial instruction, a teacher presents an instruction to the student, and the student responds to the instruction. The teacher then provides reinforcement for correct responses and corrective feedback for incorrect responses. The period of time between the delivery of reinforcement or feedback and the start of the next trial is called the inter-trial interval.

Historically, teachers have used the inter-trial interval following reinforcement to take data and prepare for the next trial before delivering the next instruction. However, recommendations to increase the speed of delivery of trials led to the minimization of the use of an inter-trial interval. The thought behind this alteration in the discrete trial is that minimizing the inter-trial interval both maximizes behavioral momentum (see chapter 2), and also maximizes the amount of instruction provided. For teachers, the elimination of the inter-trial interval creates a rapid pace of instruction in which the delivery of reinforcement or corrective feedback leads right into the delivery of the next instruction. For example, following a correct response, the teacher will quickly manipulate the materials as necessary while saying, "That was a great job touching the ball. Where is the tree?"

Another way to maximize instructional time and exposure to language is by providing "extra" information to the student within a teaching session. *Instructive feedback* is the provision of "extra" information in the context of language instruction with the hope that the extra information will help the student learn that information faster at a later time. For instance, an instructor who is teaching a child to receptively identify pictures of common objects might ask her to touch the "shoe." When she does so correctly, to provide instructive feedback the teacher could then say, "That's right, that's the shoe! A shoe goes on your foot." Though the learner is not required to repeat or respond to the extra information ("A shoe goes on your foot"), some research suggests that she will later demonstrate rapid acquisition of the question, "What goes on your foot?" because she was exposed to the extra language during instructive feedback. A small body of research has demonstrated success with this method when teaching students with autism. In essence, the teacher gets "learning for free" by including extra language in language instruction.

Functional Programming

General movements within the special education field also influence the use of language in our classrooms. We refer within this book to the importance of functional programming and focusing skill development on age-appropriate skills that will benefit students both now and in the future (chapter 6, "Quality over Quantity," and chapter 8, "Make It Meaningful"). While it is easy to see that some skills are functional, such as learning to unload the dishwasher or write one's name, other skills do not *seem* functional at face value; that is, one cannot always easily deduce how the skill will be used in the natural environment. To borrow again from a receptive language example, asking a student to select a picture of a cat from an array of three pictures may not seem immediately functional. The student may not have a cat, there may be no immediate plan to have her engage with a cat, and the word *cat* will not help her in the classroom or home environment. While the focus on the word *cat* may not seem functional, it is the process of learning that the word *cat* refers to a picture of the cat that is the functional skill being taught. This ability to discriminate between stimuli and identify a named item will eventually extend to more functional activities such as following directions to get ready to go home (e.g., get your backpack and your lunchbox) or setting the table (e.g., get a plate and a spoon). However, at its infancy, it can be difficult to make a discrimination task appear functional.

To remedy this problem, some teachers may work to improve the functionality of a program by making a task appear "contextual." To do this, they couch the task within a functional context by adding language to the task. For example, when asking a child to imitate the sound "mmm," a teacher might say, "When I eat my food, it's really yummy, and I say, 'Mmmmm.' Say 'mmmm.'" As another example, when asking a student to imitate the motor skill of touching her head, the teacher might say, "You have really long hair. Do this [touches head]." This extra language could be potentially beneficial to the student, but the main purpose it serves for the teacher is to make a task appear more functional.

Building Rapport

Perhaps most importantly, teachers incorporate language into instruction to build rapport—or a strong therapeutic connection—with their students. The field of psychology, in general, places considerable emphasis on the importance of rapport-building in treatment. Therapists who establish strong rapport with their clients are generally thought to get more buy-in from them, which can result in the client putting forth more effort in treatment and seeing a better outcome.

The field of ABA has a similar focus on rapport-building, despite the long-standing myth that ABA is a cold and emotionless science. In many programs we visit, we see teachers striving to make a connection with their students on a daily basis, playing and interacting with them with true affection. When working with children with ASD, building rapport is virtually synonymous with what is called "pairing," a process in which a teacher pairs herself with desirable and fun activities by delivering them, engaging in them, and building upon them (often with language) to make them more desirable and more fun. For instance, if a student is motivated by bouncing on a trampoline, the teacher can pair herself with the activity by giving the student access to the trampoline and then remaining as part of the activity by holding the student's hands as he jumps, and helping him jump higher than he could on his own. By pairing herself repeatedly with desirable activities such as the trampoline, the teacher becomes an agent of reinforcement and the student will be more motivated to interact and work with the teacher.

Following the oft-taught recommendation to "Make it fun!" for the learner, teachers use language to talk naturally with students during pairing sessions and also work sessions. Teachers may joke with students, and comment on fun activities with them. For some teachers, building a strong relationship with a student creates feelings of friendly affection that can be expressed through words using nicknames and terms of endearment. These nicknames, such as "friend" and "kiddo," can make the teaching session seem more natural and less formal, and also help the teacher convey the affection he or she has for the learner. Often, the use of specific terms of endearment develop within a classroom or school. A teacher who has the opportunity to work in different settings over time may find that the nicknames commonly used for students are different in each setting, but consistent across all the teachers within each setting. For instance, one classroom of teachers may consistently refer to all students as "kiddo," while another classroom calls all children "friend," and still another may call all boys "buddy" and all girls "little miss." Subsequently, the teacher may adopt these nicknames as she settles into her new role in each classroom.

What Do Problems with Language Instruction Look Like?

Ultimately, the high level of language some teachers use when instructing students with autism has well-meaning origins. Teachers who are creating a language-rich environment are doing so to optimize their learners' opportunities for language learning, make the tasks seem more functional, and establish a strong relationship with learners to enhance learning. However, in some cases, the amount of language used in instruction may interfere with learning.

Language Is Beyond Learner Comprehension

The range of learners on the autism spectrum is incredibly diverse. As was discussed earlier, the language abilities vary considerably from student to student. Some learners in classrooms are nonverbal or minimally verbal, and working hard to grasp some of the most basic concepts of language. For children who are acquiring early language and possibly still even developing readiness skills for learning such as sitting appropriately, attending to the teacher, and responding to basic instruction, the abundance of language described above may be beyond their comprehension level.

Consider the child, for instance, who is learning to touch a picture of a cat when she is told to "Touch cat." This child, although five years old, is nonverbal and has no receptive language skills to date. In this case, even using the word *touch* may be beyond her comprehension level and confusing; she may not know whether the word *touch* or *cat* or *touch cat* is the label for the picture of the cat. Many protocols for teaching auditory discrimination, such as those written by Gina Green and Laura Grow and colleagues, recommend only saying the single word *cat* to ensure that the learner is attending to the correct stimulus and not distracted by extraneous language (*touch*).

It stands to reason, then, that the same child would struggle with the following flow of language from her teacher: "I have a pet at home, and it is a cat. Touch cat. That's the cat! Cats have soft fur. Great job, kiddo! High five. Touch dog." The teacher may have carefully chosen his or her words to create a language-rich environment, increase the appearance of functionality, and build rapport as described above. However, in this situation with this particular learner, the additional language is likely incomprehensible and may only serve to make it more difficult for her to identify and use the useful information—the word *cat* and, subsequently, the word *dog*—to respond to the task.

Learners May Not Attend to the Instruction

As described above, when teachers give task demands in rapid succession and place demands in functional context, they run the risk of not clearly emphasizing the instruction for the student. For learners who have established language and can readily isolate the instruction, the use of one-word directives makes little sense and is not recommended. These learners may be able to learn language easily in context through conversation. However, for learners for whom language acquisition is more challenging, the conversational approach illustrated above may be a particular hurdle to acquisition.

Many young children with ASD are still acquiring learning readiness skills, many of which are discussed in chapter 3, "Wait for It." These students are learning how to attend and how to correctly respond to instruction. However, if they are unable to recognize that an instruction has been delivered, or isolate the relevant stimulus within the instruction, they are unlikely to respond correctly. The task of isolating the relevant stimulus becomes especially challenging in fast-paced instruction where little pause is provided between reinforcement and the delivery of the next trial, or where the pause is "filled" with extraneous language. For instance, an instructor might use a "run-on sentence" by praising a student and launching quickly into the next trial—"Wow, that's an awesome job clapping your hands, Mister Man, you're so amazing, stomp your feet." This may make it difficult or impossible for the student to isolate the instructions ("clap your hands," "stomp your feet").

Furthermore, if a student with ASD has difficulty identifying the relevant stimuli in a teacher's instruction, the extraneous words—especially if they are consistently used—may inadvertently begin to control her response to the task. As an example, to reduce problem behavior during transitions from preferred activities to work, many teachers prepare their students for the transition by counting down until it is time for a student to relinquish a preferred item. Sometimes, however, these countdowns are too short to actually prepare a student for a transition, and are stated as a phrase such as "Three, two, one, my turn." Under these circumstances, the child may begin to learn to relinquish the item when she hears, "Three, two, one" instead of responding to the relevant instruction, "My turn." While this development of stimulus control may be of little consequence in work sessions (she still hands over the item when it's time), when it comes time to generalize this skill to new settings, the child may have considerable difficulty. For example, if she is playing a game with another child and the peer says, "My turn," the student may not respond appropriately because she has not associated the phrase "My turn" with the behavior of handing a preferred item to another person.

Another specific example of extraneous language taking on controlling properties is the use of nicknames or terms of endearment in the classroom. For many parents, their child's inability to respond to his or her name by looking at the parent is one of the first red flags that their child may not be developing as expected. Lack of "response to name" is a common skill deficit for children with autism, and teaching a student to respond to his or her name is a crucial skill often included in programming. By replacing a child's name with nicknames (no matter how affectionate), the number of opportunities the child has to learn to respond to her name is greatly reduced. Further, she may learn to respond to the nickname or term of endearment instead of her own name. This inadvertent control of a nickname may be especially problematic if it is a generic name (e.g., "kiddo," "buddy") that is not used by people outside of the classroom, such as parents.

Learners Are Less Likely to Attend to Instructors

Remember the old Peanuts cartoons, where each time the teacher talks, all the students hear is "Wah wah wah wah"? When teachers use too much irrelevant language with early language learners, they risk creating a similar situation in which their students no longer attend to even the most relevant information. Essentially, a learner must put in considerable effort to isolate the words needed to complete the task when those words are couched in sentences and phrases meant to make the task functional and fun. Even if the student is able to complete the task correctly, the amount of reinforcement offered may not be worth the effort that was required to isolate the relevant information for the task. Additionally, the teacher cannot guarantee that the learner has correctly made an association between the correct word in the sentence and the stimulus, so subsequent success may be unlikely.

Unfortunately, though many teachers use language to build rapport and "pair" with their students, all that work can be undone quickly if learners no longer attend to the language of their instructors. If the effort required to respond correctly to instructors is high and students make slow progress, they may begin to avoid the work setting and the instructor associated with that setting. Further, some teachers may rely on praise as reinforcement, but when it ceases to be salient because it is slotted into a "run-on sentence" with other unfamiliar words, it may become less salient and thus not reinforcing. Praise statements may become even less valuable to a child if they are always immediately followed by another demand. Essentially, the forms of reinforcement that teachers rely on to maintain rapport and student responding may be ineffective, and student motivation and progress will slow.

Loud, Distracting Classroom Environments

One final consideration in using a high level of language when working with early language learners is whether instructors' talk contributes to a loud, distracting classroom environment. Many individuals with autism actively avoid loud noises or high levels of sensory stimulation such as are found in crowded areas and music concerts. Further, many individuals with autism demonstrate overselectivity, or the inability to focus on the intended cue in the environment to learn how to respond. For example, a child who is asked to place a fork on the table may instead select a spoon because she is not attending to the relevant features of the tableware—the curved bowl of the spoon and the tines of the fork—but is instead focusing on the handles that are identical on each. Imagine, then, a classroom of teachers and teachers' assistants working with a classroom of children with autism. If all are providing copious amounts of language in their instruction, the result can be a very loud, distracting environment. The students may have difficulty "tuning out" the instruction provided to others to focus on and respond to their own teacher's instruction.

There is certainly value in increasing the distraction inherent in a classroom, especially for students who will be transitioning to mainstream classrooms. For learners who are focusing on early language skills, however, this distraction may disrupt learning and potentially lead them to avoid the classroom setting.

What Can We Do about the Problem?

Know Your Learner

Instruction for individuals with autism is highly individualized. Because of the range of skills that students may have, teachers must be able to tailor their interventions to the needs of each student. Language instruction, and the use of language with the student, is no different. When working with a student on the spectrum, a teacher should carefully consider his or her language level. Importantly, the teacher must recognize that learners often have skills in related areas that mask their true language abilities. For example, a child with autism may be able to script, or repeat, entire conversations from a favorite TV show. Another child may be able to read words significantly above her grade level. However, the ability to script and read does not mean that the child comprehends what he or she is saying. Scripting and reading do not require comprehension or understanding, but teachers may interact with students at a level higher than they are capable because of these false indicators of well-developed language abilities.

An assessment of language abilities will be useful in identifying the student's current level of receptive and expressive language. Assessments such as the *Assessment of Basic Language and Learning Skills*, *Verbal Behavior Milestones and Placement Protocol*, and *Peabody Picture Vocabulary Tests* will provide the instructor with a general guideline of current language abilities. Maurice, Green, and Luce recommend that verbal instructions should always be provided at grade level. That is, the language used to give instructions to a learner with ASD should not exceed the language expected of a student with his or her age-equivalence.

This chapter has already discussed Maurice, Green, and Luce's recommendation that teachers should comment on their students' environment to help increase vocabulary. However, Maurice, Green, and Luce also recommend that, when talking to an individual with autism, instructors should practice the skill of *reduction*, or minimizing the amount of language used to encourage her to imitate language at her present level of language development. Commenting on the environment is important to build vocabulary, but it should be done at a level easily comprehended by the student. Again, it is important for a teacher to be aware of the child's language abilities and provide language at that level.

As the learner begins to successfully imitate, use, and respond to language at that level, instructors can begin the process of *expansion*, or slowly building up the complexity of their own language. This maximizes the learner's comprehension and provides a model for continued language development. For instance, when language instruction begins, you may focus primarily on teaching the student to label or ask for things she likes. One-word teacher directives will provide her with a clear model of language, and also ensure that the correct stimulus controls behavior without the interference of extraneous language. However, once a learner begins to imitate or respond to one-word phrases, you can build upon known vocabulary. If a student has begun to successfully identify a variety of items in the classroom when given a one-word instruction such as "book," "backpack," or "lunchbox," you may begin to expand the length of the instruction to "touch book," "get backpack," or "close lunchbox." When a learner expressively labels "TV" while turning on the television, you may expand on this by commenting, "TV on." As children age and their language continues to develop, their length of utterances can increase, and you can introduce more complex language into instructional periods.

Emphasize Instructions

When working with early language learners who may also still be acquiring learning readiness skills, teachers should ensure that they emphasize the instructions they provide for tasks. This does not mean that you should deliver the instruction with the same intonation, volume, and affect during each trial; this will only reinforce stereotypes of ABA that portray instructors and their learners as robotic. Rather, you should vary your intonation, volume, and affect when giving instructions, but limit extraneous language, as described above. This increases the likelihood that the learner will attend to the relevant stimuli in following directions or responding to language. Again, the level of language used in the instruction should match the student's present level of language development.

Additionally, instructors may make use of the inter-trial interval to mark the distinction between praise or corrective feedback and the delivery of the next instruction. This momentary pause between the two components of an effective discrete trial will increase the salience of both the instruction and the instructor's response to the instruction.

In this pause, you can collect data and also target other goals such as identifying student motivation and establishing student attending (see chapter 3, "Wait for It").

As a child's language develops, the instructor can be looser with the pace of instruction and the inclusion of extraneous language. Indeed, studies have shown that teachers sometimes get "learning for free" by including extra language in work sessions, as in instructive feedback. However, as teachers increase the use of language in instruction, they should continuously monitor student comprehension and ability to respond to the most relevant language required for a task. For instance, if a student transitions to an inclusion classroom where she will be exposed to high levels of language from the teacher and peers, the teacher or a teacher assistant should periodically ask her to repeat or rephrase the instructions of the teacher, or the content of a lesson, to ensure that she truly comprehends the language used in the academic tasks presented.

One additional note regarding emphasizing the instruction for learners: Be cautious of giving instructions when they are not needed. In some situations, the task or activity will set the occasion for the completion of a specific behavior, and an instruction is not necessary. For instance, if a student has finished using the bathroom, eventually one would hope that she would wash her hands without the instruction "Wash your hands." After a child has learned to wash her hands, the instructor should focus on getting her to wash her hands without being told to do so. Similarly, if a student is working at a restaurant and one of her tasks is to set the table for the next customer, the instructor working with her should not need to tell her to "set the table" at each empty table; the clean, empty table should prompt the student to set out the tableware. In situations such as these, teachers should recognize the importance of allowing naturally occurring stimuli in the environment to control the behavior rather than have it be controlled by their instruction.

Connect in Other Ways

Teachers who are asked to minimize the amount of language they use in the classroom may feel stripped of their personality when working with students with ASD. They may feel as though they will be unable to connect with students because they will be unable to insert humor and affection into their interactions with those students. However, these teachers must remember that if the learner is not at a developmental level at which she could comprehend or respond to the language the teacher uses, no matter how humorous or affectionate, her efforts will be lost on him. Rapport could be damaged, and, at worst, the student could fail to make progress.

Teachers can certainly connect and relate to students with ASD nonverbally while also targeting the language at the learner's level. A teacher's creativity will be showcased in the ways in which she can contrive fun activities and tasks to naturally motivate her students to express and respond to language. Her fun-loving nature can be demonstrated in the enthusiastic way she delivers reinforcement to the learner. High-fives, smiles, hair tousles, and tickles—if enjoyed and appropriate for the child's age—can convey just as much affection and build rapport more easily for many children than the use of nicknames and verbal praise.

Summing Up

The profound language deficits of many learners with autism will urge any teacher to focus heavily on language programming. Influences from within the field, such as recommendations to create a language-rich environment and functional programming, as well as the teacher's desire to establish a connection with his or her students, may drive the teacher to saturate the student's environment with language. While some learners with autism who struggle only with pragmatic language deficits may be able to learn well in this environment, early language learners may have considerable difficulty isolating relevant words to help develop their vocabulary and respond appropriately to the language they encounter. Teachers should be mindful of the level of language development of each learner and present language instruction at a level that provides appropriate models for language while maximizing student comprehension. Modulating the level of teacher language and the pace of instruction will help an early learner better attend to relevant language.

Teachers can maintain a sense of connection to their students through nonverbal language and by developing creative, fun approaches to teaching that keep students engaged and motivated. Ensuring that students are engaged by meeting them at their language level will help build solid language skills that will form the groundwork for continued language development as they grow.

SELF-ASSESSMENT: Do You Need to "Talk Less"?

Observe teaching interactions within the classroom and respond to the following questions:

1. What is the essential language in this situation?

   _____

2. Is there any language that is extraneous? If so, what language?

   _____

3. Is the extraneous language one of the following?

   ☐ Extra language to make the demand contextual

   ☐ Classroom and school catchphrases

   ☐ Nicknames

   ☐ Run-on sentences during the inter-trial interval

4. Does the learner comprehend the language being used? How do you know? Does it matter?

   _____

   _____

5. Is all of the language used for the learner's benefit?

   _____

6. Is the language present for someone else's benefit?

   ☐ The instructor's own benefit

   ☐ The benefit of another observer

7. What impact does the extraneous language have on the learner?

   _____

   _____

8. Is there excess language from other children or instructors in the environment? Should this be addressed and how?

_____

_____

_____

9. Does the instructor pause between praising one response and presenting the next instruction?

_____

10. Does the instructor provide unnecessary instructions?

_____

11. Does the instructor use simple and salient instructions or unnatural instructions? Explain.

_____

_____

_____

12. Should the instruction be made more natural for this learner or situation? Why or why not?

_____

_____

_____

6 | Quality over Quantity

Catriona Francis

Angela Brown has been providing early intervention services in the homes of young children with ASD for five years. She received her training at a program providing services using applied behavior analysis (ABA) and feels competent working with young children. Angela is aware of the research literature that has shown that Early Intensive Behavioral Intervention (EIBI) can produce developmental gains and increase the possibility of a child requiring less intensive services later on in his or her childhood.

Rodrigo is a three-year-old boy with whom Angela has been working for the last six months. Although Rodrigo shows an interest in a few toys, Angela has difficulty trying to establish those items as motivators for him to participate in teaching sessions and comply with instructions. Angela knows that her time with Rodrigo is important and that her goal is to practice the skills he is working on as many times as possible each session to ensure his progress on those skills. Rodrigo's mother, Isabella Rivera, is present during most of Angela's sessions with Rodrigo. Isabella has also expressed often that it is essential that Rodrigo practice his skills frequently and that sessions should be filled with as much teaching and as few breaks as possible.

As time goes on, Angela is growing concerned with the quality of the learning opportunities she is providing Rodrigo. It is difficult to get him to attend to her, and she finds herself having to prompt him through the teaching trials to ensure his compliance with her instructions. At the suggestion of her colleagues, Angela has been using a quicker pace of instruction, as well as interspersals (mixing in maintenance tasks that Rodrigo has already mastered with current learning targets). This has resulted in some success getting practice opportunities in because the pace of the overall session has increased. Angela continues to have concerns, however, because although she is providing many teaching opportunities, she does not feel that Rodrigo is benefitting from all of them. In addition, Rodrigo is not acquiring skills any faster than before. Angela decides to bring her concerns to the rest of the educational team at their next meeting to see if there is a way to maximize the benefit to Rodrigo.

Overview of the Issue: Intensive Behavioral Intervention

Research supports the fact that intensive behavioral intervention using ABA results in significant improvement for individuals with ASD compared with non-intensive treatment. The results of a landmark study of EIBI, the UCLA Young Autism Project by Ivar Lovaas, showed that individuals who received forty hours of intensive treatment received several important benefits. First, they were far more likely to make gains in their IQ score, and second, they were more likely to be integrated into a regular education classroom than individuals who either received fewer than ten hours of one-to-one behavioral treatment or received treatment in other programs that did not provide intensive behavioral treatment.

A number of additional research studies in the years following Lovaas's article have supported these findings:

- The May Institute Study (Anderson et al., 1987) indicated that children with ASD who had not previously been making progress in their preschool programs began to show gains in skills and reduction of maladaptive behavior in response to fifteen to twenty-five hours a week of intensive behavioral teaching from trained teachers as well as their parents.
- The Murdoch Early Intervention Program study (Birnbrauer & Leach, 1993) found similarly that children who received an average of 18.72 hours a week of home-based one-to-one intensive behavioral instruction were more likely to make developmental gains than those in a control group who did not receive behavioral intervention. These gains included improving their IQ score from being untestable to scoring at least 80 and improving on language and adaptive behavior tests.

■ Sheinkopf & Siegel (1998) found similar results in their study of home-based behavioral treatment for children with autism. Children who received intensive behavioral treatment had higher average mental age estimates and IQ estimates after treatment than the individuals in the control group that they were matched with at the beginning of the study. Individuals who received intensive treatment were also rated as having less severe autistic symptoms after treatment.

A 2009 review of more recent research continues to support the broad benefits of intensive behavioral intervention (Eldevik et al., 2009). There does not appear from the research to be any disagreement about the effectiveness of early intensive behavioral services. In fact, the benefits of intervention using the principles of applied behavior analysis have been demonstrated for individuals of all ages. Given this information, it is not difficult to understand why parents, as strong advocates for their children, and professionals, as eager service providers, want to see as much instruction fit into each therapy session or school day as possible.

How Intensive Is Intensive Enough?

What is missing in the research, however, is a clear description of what makes services "intensive." There is general agreement among the majority of ABA clinicians on the minimum number of hours (greater than ten per week), and there is a general consensus that time spent in intervention should be filled with as many learning opportunities as possible to allow for repeated practice of target skills. However, in the absence of research to inform more specific guidelines, a great deal is left to those providing services to structure instructional sessions.

Many ABA providers or teachers may develop models of service delivery that focus on certain components of teaching to make intensity of instruction a priority, and these service models are established as trends in the field. In many cases, teaching trends are based on a sound theoretical position and good preliminary evidence, and the resulting practices become synonymous with "best practice." This is similar to the process described in chapter 2, "Don't Give It Away," in which the practitioners in the field started focusing more on manding (requesting).

However, there are times when trends within the field influence the structure of teaching sessions even though nobody has done a careful evaluation of the impact those changes have on a *specific learner*. This happens when there is some evidence that a particular way of working with children is effective *in general*, and then clinicians adopt this way of working with all children, without more extensive research or individualized evaluation. There are some other trends that may inadvertently emphasize *quantity* of instruction, and that can have an impact on the quality of instruction if they are not carefully monitored. Examples that the authors of this book have seen include the following:

- a focus on fast-paced instruction,
- the use of interspersals (mixed known and unknown material in teaching),
- the use of percent correct data, and
- instructor training that focuses on pace, interspersal, and number of learning trials *rather than* on teaching outcomes.

It is important to remember that these aspects of teaching are not, in and of themselves, problematic. In fact, these strategies have been introduced and disseminated on the basis of good clinical outcomes and preliminary evidence. However, when these strategies are not balanced with other considerations and are not individually evaluated, they may create problems in the quality of instruction.

The first of these, a focus on fast-paced instruction, may be an outgrowth of the use of behavioral momentum (which is described in chapter 2). It can lead to more learning opportunities, an important part of intensive instruction, but the resulting learning opportunities are less natural. This is because it is easier to practice one thing multiple times out of context than to plan for more naturally occurring practice opportunities. To read more on the concept of natural and embedded learning opportunities, see chapter 8, "Make It Meaningful."

Often, the focus on instructional pace and behavioral momentum also involves the use of what is called interspersal: mixing new and mastered skills in the same teaching session. Remember, *behavioral momentum* relies on "high probability" requests to build up momentum to increase the chances of having a child respond to a "low probability" request. In a teaching session, you can see how a "high probability request" (one that has a high probability of being answered correctly) can be considered a known skill, and a low probability request might be a new or harder skill. So, if a child is working on the skill of imitating words, and he has already learned how to imitate sounds, an instructor might ask him to repeat a number of familiar and easy sounds, "ah," "buh," "mmm," before then asking him to say "o-pen," a two-syllable word.

The way student progress is measured may also play a role in the development of some of these issues. If the progress is measured by percent correct or percent of opportunities, then there must be a higher number of opportunities for those data to make sense. Some programs using percent data to evaluate student progress might have a rule that the instructor needs to have provided at least ten opportunities in order to "count" the data. Instructors may push to get as many trials or opportunities as possible for this reason.

Most quality instructional programs train their staff to perform at specific levels of competence and often measure these aspects of staff behavior. For example, a supervisor may watch an instructor working with a child and count the number of learning opportunities provided, and count the number of new and mastered items presented within the session. Sometimes, a program may unintentionally focus on staff behavior without also paying enough attention to student outcome. In other words, staff members are evaluated on whether they are quick enough or provide enough learning opportunities, without evaluating them on the effectiveness and meaningfulness of those opportunities. While the focus of these types of training measures is to make sure instructors are maximizing instructional time, an important goal, it is a problem if the outcome for the student is overlooked because of the focus on staff behavior.

What Do Problems with Intensive Intervention Look Like?

The problem comes when the quantity of learning opportunities provided is the *only* measure of the intensity of an instructional session. If the quality of those learning opportunities is not also examined, there is a risk that interventions will be less effective. Problems related to focusing exclusively on the quantity of learning opportunities, without consideration of the quality of those opportunities, include the following:

- Instructions are delivered when the learner is not ready to learn.
- Compliance and performance only occur at an unnatural pace.
- Learning opportunities are isolated rather than contextual.
- More time is spent teaching skills than is necessary.

These problems are discussed in detail in the sections below.

Delivering Instructions When the Learner Is Not Ready to Learn

When the primary focus of a behavioral therapist or teacher is to begin instruction as quickly as possible and to provide as many learning opportunities as possible, there is a risk that he or she will not focus sufficiently on ensuring that the learner is ready to learn. A learner is more likely to engage in a high quality response when he is motivated to engage in the behavior (see chapter 1, "Make It Worthwhile") and when he is attending to the relevant information present in the environment (see chapter 3, "Wait for It"). Presenting instructions to a child who is not motivated or is not paying attention to either the instructor or the materials in front of him is not likely to result in a quality learning opportunity. In fact, doing so can result in the use of prompts (see chapter 4, "Hands Off") to ensure that the learner completes the task he is given. Think about the outcome of an interaction in which a teacher helps a student comply with a task that he either is not motivated to complete or cannot complete because he did not pay attention to the instruction. In this situation, while the learner may have learned that he cannot escape the task by refusing to comply—a possible goal in terms of teaching appropriate behavior—from a skill-acquisition perspective, he has not learned the skill itself.

Are Skills Missing? For some learners, these readiness skills are missing from their repertoire. Formal instruction is needed to establish basic learning-to-learn skills. Before a child can benefit from any form of instruction, he must be taught to cooperate with an instructor's request. He must learn that he will receive access to immediate rewards when he does so. He must also learn how to sit, look at, and pay attention to the teacher and materials, and respond to feedback (Leaf, McEachin, Taubman, *A Work in Progress* companion series). For these children, the instructional session initially should be devoted to teaching these skills so that they can benefit from further instruction. More on this later and in chapter 3.

Is Motivation a Problem? For other learners, learning-to-learn skills may be in their repertoire, but a lack of motivation or other distractions in the environment, including their own stereotyped behavior, may interfere with their ability to learn other skills at any particular moment. For these learners, instructors should ensure that they are motivated and attending before initiating a teaching interaction. As teachers, we must look for behavior that indicates a child's readiness for learning prior to beginning instruction. Once we have determined a potential reinforcer for a learner and he is sitting down, looking at us, and not engaging in any other interfering behaviors, we can expect that he is ready to give us his highest quality response and is the most likely to learn from the teaching interaction.

In either case, whether a child is missing early skills that will allow him to benefit from intensive instruction or he has the skills in his repertoire but is indicating in the moment that he is not ready to benefit from the learning interaction, instruction should not begin. The time that the teacher or therapist takes to ensure that a child is ready for learning will likely decrease the overall quantity of learning opportunities. At the end of such a session, the overall number of learning opportunities may be less than it would have been if instruction had begun right away. The quality of the interactions, however, will be increased and the outcome for the student potentially improved.

Compliance and Performance Only Occur at an Unnatural Pace

If we use a quick instructional pace or interspersals (mixing in previously acquired tasks with new tasks) to ensure a student receives as many learning opportunities as possible, we must also be aware of the potential problems we may be creating. Some people with ASD, as a result of their exposure to quick-paced instruction and the use of interspersals, come to rely on that structure in order to comply with instructions or perform correctly on the task they are learning. Without this structure, they have difficulty complying with more difficult demands (ones they are still learning to do).

While the use of interspersals and a quick pace may potentially benefit children with ASD by providing them with frequent practice of both previously acquired skills and target skills, those approaches do not prepare them for the more natural pace of the real world.

The outcome of instruction should be a learner's ability to perform a skill independently in a more natural context. If, by the nature of our approach, we are preventing this from happening, we are not providing quality services.

Instructors sometimes also use fast-paced instruction to compete with or prevent interfering behaviors. Presenting instructions rapidly prevents "down time" during which a learner may engage in interfering behaviors such as motor or vocal stereotypy. The downside of using this approach is that the individual with ASD is not being taught to sit appropriately in order to benefit from instruction as much as he is being prevented from engaging in interfering behaviors. As we mentioned before, it is when a student is sitting appropriately and looking to the teacher for information on what he should do that he is most likely to give a high quality response. A slower-paced, more deliberate approach to instruction that involves establishing motivation and then expecting readiness behaviors prior to beginning a teaching interaction may result in a better outcome for learners than an approach that focuses primarily on presenting high numbers of learning opportunities.

Presentation of Isolated Rather Than Contextual Learning Opportunities

Another problem that can occur if we focus primarily on quantity of learning opportunities provided is that we may neglect to provide those learning opportunities within a functional context (refer to chapter 8, Make It Meaningful). As we have been discussing, measuring how productive an instructional session is by the number of programs or number of trials completed regardless of whether or not the learner benefited from any of the teaching interactions has the potential to diminish the quality of the session. When the focus of an instructional session is on presenting as many opportunities as possible for each target skill, there may be less focus on how meaningfully each teaching opportunity is presented. Because of the additional time required to set up a learning opportunity in a functional context, teachers or behavioral therapists who are focused on ensuring large numbers of practice opportunities may opt for less functional materials that are easier to assemble quickly rather than taking the time to provide a contextually relevant opportunity.

Consider two alternatives for teaching a child how to tie his shoe. In the first scenario, you give the child the opportunity to change out of a pair of sandals and into a pair of sneakers that need to be tied in order to go outside to play on a swing, a highly preferred activity. Compare that to a second scenario in which you place a toddler shoe on the desk in front of the child to tie. The second child is provided with fifteen consecutive opportunities to practice tying the shoe on his desk, and each time he successfully completes the task, he gets a token that he can trade in later to play a preferred game on a tablet. In the first scenario, the child is provided with a more contextually relevant opportunity and one that is rewarded by natural contingencies of reinforcement (access to the swing). This opportunity requires planning and more time to complete (additional time is added to the actual tying of the shoes because the child must first remove his sandals and then be provided with time for the highly preferred activity of swinging). The second scenario requires far less planning and can be repeated a number of times in a short period of time.

The question of whether fewer, more contextual opportunities to practice a skill or many more isolated opportunities to practice a skill results in quicker acquisition is an empirical one that should be evaluated for each student. It is important, however, to stress that just because it is possible to provide more isolated practice opportunities of a skill does not in itself guarantee the quality of those interactions or that the learner will master the skill more quickly. We are also not saying that non-contextual or repeated practice must be avoided. However, it is important to stress that it should only be one aspect of instruction, and one that is used only as needed.

More Time Is Spent Teaching Skills Than Is Necessary

Very few, if any, teachers or parents would disagree that children learn things more quickly when they are paying attention. It is for this reason that we suggest looking more closely at the concept of quantity when we are talking about providing behavioral intervention. Our goal as professionals is to teach a skill well in as little time as possible. Ensuring quality teaching interactions in which a learner is actively engaged is the only way to do this. Repeatedly exposing a child to practice opportunities without ensuring that he is ready to be an active participant in the learning is not likely to be successful in achieving our desired outcome. To ensure that we do not spend more time teaching skills than is necessary, we must address the concepts of quality along with quantity.

In any program using the principles of applied behavior analysis, data analysis should be ongoing so instructors can make programmatic changes as needed in order to ensure learner progress. The success of behavioral intervention should be measured in terms of outcomes for the learner. If we are to claim that providing many practice opportunities is what a particular child needs in order to acquire skills, we must have data to support that approach. It is important that we evaluate the best way to teach each individual learner. Neglecting to do so can result in more time spent teaching a particular skill than is necessary.

It may be the case that less frequent, more contextual opportunities to practice skills would result in faster acquisition for some learners. Using this approach for certain students would potentially result in faster generalization of the skill to more natural contexts. Because our goal should be for our learners to respond appropriately in situations that present themselves naturally as part of their daily lives, we must ensure that the way we instruct them does not prevent this from happening. Teaching should not end until a learner is able to perform a skill in the environment with natural contingencies of reinforcement. We must make sure that our effort to provide a large number of learning opportunities does not result in practice opportunities that are so different from real-world situations that we have to spend additional time teaching learners how to respond in the real world.

What Can We Do about the Problem?

Many people with ASD do require a large number of opportunities to practice skills before they acquire them. Those opportunities, however, must be of high quality. Fortunately, there are ways to ensure that we are striking a balance between quantity of learning opportunities presented during intensive behavioral intervention and the quality of each of those opportunities. The following sections suggest three ways to ensure that quality of teaching interactions is considered along with quantity:

- Evaluate whether a learner is ready to learn before teaching him.

- Plan for meaningful learning opportunities.
- Consider alternatives for collecting and reporting data.

Evaluate Whether a Learner Is Ready to Learn Before Teaching

When a professional is working with a child for the first time, he or she must evaluate whether the learner has the skills necessary to benefit from instruction. Teachers and therapists must complete formal assessments to determine if the child has the skills in his repertoire to be ready to learn. Ron Leaf, John McEachin, and Mitch Taubman list the following "Learning How to Learn" skills in their book, *A Work in Progress Companion Series* (Leaf, McEachin & Taubman, 2012):

- Attending behaviors (orienting to the instructor, establishing eye contact with the instructor prior to instruction, looking at the instructor while responding, etc.)
- Returning reinforcers (complying with instruction to return a preferred item)
- Reduce fidgeting
- Waiting (waiting for access to a preferred item or for attention from another individual, waiting in line at a fast food restaurant, etc.)
- Cooperating and responding
- Learning from feedback: contingencies (learning to use feedback given by a teacher and to change a response if feedback indicates the response was incorrect)
- Responding to prompts
- Discrimination training (understanding what something is and is not—e.g., when presented with two objects, only points to the correct one when given its label, never to the other item)

If a child is missing any of these foundation skills, it is imperative that he or she receive formal instruction to establish them.

Once a child with ASD has demonstrated his readiness to learn, teachers and therapists must learn to be responsive to him in the moment. A child who has the skills and motivation to do so should indicate his readiness for learning by sitting appropriately and looking to the teacher in order to find out what he should do next. A skilled teacher will spend time reinforcing this "readiness" behavior to ensure the child engages in it consistently. If the child is engaged in interfering behavior such as motor or vocal stereotypy or is not looking at the instructor, the teacher should realize that he would not benefit from instruction in the moment. Rather than beginning to teach, the instructor should focus on identifying something motivating to the learner and working to establish attending behaviors prior to beginning instruction.

A skilled teacher who slows down instruction to wait for a student to indicate he is ready will ultimately see him engage in higher quality responses indicative of his skill level. It is not how many learning opportunities a teacher presents, but how many learning opportunities the learner benefits from that makes learning interactions effective.

Plan for Meaningful Learning Opportunities

As clinicians and teachers, we have to be thoughtful about how we capture or contrive practice opportunities. Removing the pressure to achieve a minimum number of practice opportunities when targeting a skill for a learner does not remove the work for us. We should spend a great deal of time planning a student's schedule to ensure that we take advantage of naturally occurring opportunities to teach target skills. We must also plan to insert activities into the daily schedule within which opportunities to practice skills will take place. A well-planned instructional session should provide frequent opportunities to practice skills in meaningful ways.

It is important to mention that the idea of presenting lots and lots of opportunities to practice skills is not in itself problematic. Any learner would benefit from a skilled teacher who is able to provide a large number of learning opportunities that are also high in quality. The problem arises when teachers or therapists use quantity as the only measure of how productive their work session was. Fewer, more meaningful opportunities may be preferable to many less meaningful opportunities. For example, if a teenager is learning to cut his own food, would he benefit more from cutting his own hotdog at lunchtime before he eats it (relatively few opportunities to practice cutting) or cutting a roll of play dough throughout the day (repeated opportunities to practice)? It may be the case that a learner would acquire the skill of cutting more quickly practicing the skill less frequently but more meaningfully. Ideally, however, his teacher would be able to present a larger number of meaningful opportunities and would work with the teen's parents to ensure that he has multiple items that require cutting in his lunch each day.

In addition to considering the context within which a learning opportunity is presented when creating meaningful opportunities, we should consider the learner's role in the interaction. Opportunities to practice a skill will also have more meaning for the student if he is actively engaged in the response. Consider the benefit of a child engaging in two or three high quality independent responses versus ten opportunities during which he is less motivated and is prompted by a teacher. Often, a student is more likely to see the benefit of a skill that is presented contextually and functionally. It is then that he is more likely to show his readiness to learn and be an active participant in the process. We are not interested in whether students simply comply with an instruction (which could mean prompted compliance). Instead, we want students to be engaged actively and to learn from the interaction.

Consider Alternatives for Data Collection and Reporting

Within the field of applied behavior analysis, data are collected to ensure that a student is making progress and to ensure that it is the intervention we have applied that is resulting in positive change for the individual. Percent correct or percent independent data are frequently used in teaching contexts. For example, we might find that a child responds correctly 80 percent of the time when asked to get his backpack from his locker at school. To accurately represent a child's performance with percent data, a skill must be practiced a large number of times. For example, if a student only had two opportunities to get his backpack during the day, the data from each day could not be converted to a percentage. Percentage data makes much more sense when it is applied to skills like reading words, where a student might read 27 out of 30 words correctly, which would be 90 percent. For this reason, we should consider whether converting data to a percentage makes sense for a specific skill.

Given our suggestion that fewer, more meaningful opportunities may benefit a learner (to be evaluated for each learner, of course), it may be appropriate to choose a data collection and reporting practice that does not require completing a large number of trials of each skill. For example, the use of single opportunity data, in which each opportunity (data point) is evaluated on its own, does not require that data points be combined into an overall percent. In the example above, using single opportunity data, we might find that a child responds correctly on four out of five consecutive opportunities when asked to get his backpack from his locker.

There are a variety of methods of taking data about a student's performance and tracking that data to evaluate progress. The most common methods include:

- Trial by trial data: the instructor records every trial or opportunity for the student to perform the skill and the data are converted to a percent across many opportunities
- Single opportunity data: the instructor records each opportunity but tracks them individually
- Trials to criterion data: the instructor records the number of times the student practices the skill before it is performed at criterion levels (for example, the instructor reports that a child was able to meet the criteria specified for mastery for a particular skill after 75 teaching trials)
- Probe data: the instructor takes data on intermittent opportunities for the student to perform the skill without prompts (for example, at the end of a week of teaching, the instructor provides a learner with one opportunity to perform a skill without any prompts to evaluate the effectiveness of the teaching on the days prior)

Removing the need for an arbitrarily determined minimum number of practice opportunities for each skill, or, an impractically high number of learning opportunities, can allow teachers to focus on the quality of each learning opportunity. We would like to encourage teachers to teach skills well by planning for as many meaningful practice opportunities as possible. We discourage teachers from forcing multiple practice opportunities just to be able to convert the learner's performance into a percentage. We recommend that professionals avoid starting with a data type and constructing their work session around it. Instead, clinicians should think about how to teach a skill best, and then select a data type that will help measure progress most accurately.

Summing Up

Our goal as educators and behavior analysts working with individuals on the autism spectrum is to teach skills that will increase independence and promote participation in everyday life. The intensity of the services we provide is a key component to our success. A careful examination of how we define intensive services is needed if we are to have the impact we wish to have on the individuals with whom we work. We encourage both parents and professionals to think beyond quantity of learning opportunities when they are evaluating behavioral intervention services. Ultimately, a program should be evaluated based not on how much the teacher was able to accomplish in an instructional session but on how much the individual receiving the instruction learned.

By offering this chapter as a guide, we hope to encourage a deeper examination of behavioral intervention services with increased attention paid to readying learners to learn and then providing them with the best quality learning opportunities possible.

SELF-ASSESSMENT: Are You Emphasizing Quantity at the Expense of Quality?

Questions to ask to determine how "Quality vs. Quantity" might be a factor in a learning situation.

1. Does the learner appear ready to learn or participate in the activity? *What do you see that indicates this?*

_____

_____

2. What is the pace of the instruction for this skill/activity?

_____

_____

3. How is the instructional rate being established in the current scenario? *Is the pace natural? Is the pace appropriate? Why or why not?*

_____

_____

_____

4. Based on the task observed, what are the most relevant qualities of the student's performance? Is it most important how accurate the response is, how reliable the response is, how independent the response is, how long the response can be maintained?

_____

_____

_____

_____

5. What data collection strategies would best capture the quality identified in question 4?

_____

_____

6. What are some other possibilities for data collection? Discuss pros and cons for each.

_____

_____

_____

_____

7. How many learning opportunities occurred during the scenario?

_____

_____

8. What was the quality of the learning opportunities that occurred? _Was prompting used effectively? Was the child attending to the instructor and materials? Did the learner appear to be actively engaged in the teaching interaction?_

_____

_____

_____

_____

9. Was the instructor presenting isolated opportunities or contextual ones? _Was this appropriate?_

_____

_____

10. Are there other ways those learning opportunities might have been presented?

_____

_____

7 | Individualize

Robert LaRue

Alexandra is a new staff person working in a school for students with developmental disabilities. She enjoys her job and likes interacting with the students with ASD in her classroom. Ms. Davis, the teacher in the classroom, has all eight of the preadolescent students in the class working on the same goals each day and rotating among work stations in the room. They work on coin identification, envelope stuffing, shredding paper, and identifying colors from an array. While some students do well with the tasks, others seem to really struggle.

Alexandra decides to ask the teacher why the goals are all the same. Ms. Davis tells her that this is an "autism classroom" and that these are functional goals that are important to the students. She tells Alexandra that one benefit is that once staff members have learned to implement these programs, they can work with all of the students in the class. In addition, all of the materials are already present, which saves time and resources. Alexandra thanks the teacher for her time, but something still doesn't feel right to her.

Overview of the Issue: What Is individualization?

The term *individualization* is commonly encountered in educational settings. We often hear about individualized education programs (IEPs) and individual habilitation plans (IHPs) to address the needs of students. At its core, individualization refers to the act of personalization. It involves taking measures to modify something so as to meet the special requirements of a specific person.

The U.S. Department of Education defines individualization as "instruction that is paced to the learning needs of different learners. Learning goals are the same for all students, but students can progress through the material at different speeds according to their learning needs."

The Individuals with Disabilities Education Act (IDEA, 1991) and its most recent reauthorization, the Individuals with Disabilities Education Improvement Act (IDEIA, 2004), mandate the use of individualized education programs (IEPs) for meeting the unique educational needs of each student. These pieces of legislation address the educational needs of school-aged children with disabilities. IDEA/IDEIA mandates that students should have goals that are individualized to their specific pattern of strengths and needs and that these goals be addressed in the least restrictive environment possible.

The concept of individualization is particularly important as it relates to autism spectrum disorders. While people with autism share a common diagnosis, no two students who are on the autism spectrum are the same. Patterns of strengths and deficits vary widely depending on the individual.

Intervention strategies may differ in effectiveness depending on the characteristics of each individual with ASD. For example, a ten-year-old student with many near age-level cognitive skills would have different needs than a ten-year-old student with ASD who has more significant impairments in learning. The first student may need tutoring for math, note-taking assistance, and social skills training to help her interact with her mainstream peers. On the other hand, the second student with more significant learning challenges may need highly structured instruction (e.g., discrete trial instruction), training to use an augmentative communication device, and a behavior intervention plan to control challenging behavior (e.g., aggression or self-injury). The key is to identify these differences and tailor instructional strategies to the specific needs of individual learners.

What Do Problems with Individualization Look Like?

Most experts agree that individuals on the autism spectrum benefit from individualized instruction. However, little agreement exists on what is meant by individualization and how it is achieved in educational settings. While the goal should be for each student to have a unique program tailored to his or her specific needs, this is often not the case. Unfortunately, intervention is often "individualized like all of the other ASD students." In other words, programming is individualized relative to typically functioning students (students without ASD), but not personalized to a specific person. For example, several classrooms may implement programming in the way described at the beginning of the chapter. That is, programs may have a single curriculum for all students with ASD, regardless of the students' individual learning needs. Or, in some public schools, there may be a variety of special education classrooms geared to students with different levels of functioning, with the curricula more or less following the curriculum for general education students. In this case, students with ASD are often fit into one of the existing programs.

This failure to properly individualize instruction can lead to a number of problems for students with ASD, such as slow progress, failure to progress, or even regression. When students are provided with poorly individualized services and education, it results in poorer outcomes for those students.

Where Does the Problem Come From?

While there is little argument about the wide range of differences among students on the autism spectrum and the different ways they may acquire skills, programs and schools often struggle with individualizing instruction. There are a number of reasons for this state of affairs.

In many cases, teachers have not had the opportunity to be trained in sound assessment procedures. Teachers are often taught to implement general teaching procedures, but are not given strategies to adjust them if needed. For example, an instructor may be taught to implement discrete trial instruction (DTI). Subsequently, the instructor implements DTI in the exact same way she first learned to use it for every student she works with.

A second reason that people do not individualize is that individualization is harder. Good individualization requires a considerable amount of effort from teachers. To properly individualize instruction, teachers may be required to conduct assessments, create materials, and train people to implement protocols. With so many demands on their time, it is not surprising that teachers may revert to strategies that have worked with other students in the past.

A third reason practitioners fail to individualize is cost efficiency. Think about it: if all students have the same or similar goals, all of the necessary materials are readily available. Less training is required because once a staff member is trained to implement a program, he or she can work with several students. In some settings, it might also mean that fewer instructors are needed, if the instructors are able to teach many students the same skills. Less individualization may mean that staff members don't need to be available to pull students out of the group to work on skills individually. In some of these scenarios, insufficient individualization can be a consequence of larger scale organizational and funding challenges.

Additionally, programmatic bias can lead to failures of individualization. In many cases, schools or programs may have established "models" or "protocols" that do not allow for individualization. For example, some programs may only teach communication in the form of sign language to the exclusion of other communication intervention strategies (e.g., picture exchange, augmentative devices). Take, for instance, a young student with ASD who has little or no communicative ability. There may be several ways to teach him to communicate, but some strategies may be more effective. If the student struggles with visual discrimination (i.e., he struggles with choosing items from an array), using an augmentative device or picture exchange communication system may be contraindicated. In this case, sign language may be an appropriate option. On the other hand, if a student struggles with repetitive behavior (e.g., hand flapping) or needs visual supports to communicate, augmentative devices or picture exchange may be preferable to sign language.

Finally, challenges in creating meaningfully individualized instruction may be the result of external pressure on schools to produce certain outcomes related to standardized testing and universal benchmarks. Some schools require that certain subjects or topics be taught to certain grades so that the students will be prepared for tests, and there may be quite rigid expectations that a certain number of objectives be covered every week or month. These expectations are often generated in response to education policies and initiatives at the state or federal level.

It is important to note that these problems are not necessarily the fault of the teachers working with students with ASD. Teachers and practitioners often have a multitude of responsibilities and limited time to accomplish tasks. Teachers are often not trained to individualize instruction, and efficient models for doing so have not been made available to them.

What Can We Do about the Problem?

As a general rule, we should be individualizing instruction for all students. The best way to do this is to conduct systematic assessments and to directly test the effectiveness of intervention procedures.

Use Systematic Assessments

A number of systematic assessments exist to help guide practitioners in selecting appropriate individualized goals. Among the most commonly used are the Verbal Behavior Milestones Assessment and Placement Program (VB-MAPP; Sundberg, 2008) and the Assessment of Basic Language and Learning Skills – Revised (ABLLS-R; Partington, 2008). These tools encompass skills from early childhood through adulthood, and are therefore useful for evaluating current performance, next steps, and future goals. These kinds of assessments are particularly useful for identifying students' strengths and weaknesses. These instruments provide a running log of the skills that have been acquired and skills in need of teaching, which is vital when planning individualized instruction.

These tests are generally conducted by observing the students to see what skills they do or do not demonstrate. Assessments can be conducted regularly to monitor progress (e.g., once a year). These assessments are best conducted with input from both parents and professionals to gain a complete understanding of a student's specific strengths and deficits. The results from the assessments can be used to design an IEP to ensure that proper goals are targeted.

Once a student's deficits have been identified, teachers should compare the results to goals that are currently being addressed in the classroom. In the event that the identified deficits are not being targeted, the curriculum can be adjusted to include new goals. One of the great things about measures such as the ABLLS-R or the VB-MAPP is that the assessments can help to create a road map to addressing larger, more complex goals. In the event that a teacher is unsure about how to teach a specific skill, he or she may seek out additional training or other professionals who can assist (e.g., a Board Certified Behavior Analyst).

For example, imagine you have conducted an assessment such as the ABLLS-R. The assessment reveals that James has difficulty manding (requesting) items that are out of sight. No one has previously identified this as a problem, since James has always been able to request items that he can see and it had not occurred to parents and staff that this was a deficit. Based on this information, the teacher could add a goal to teach James to request items that are out of sight. Staff could start by holding preferred items within sight and having James request them. The next step may be to hold the items under/behind the desk and have him request the items. Staff could then teach James to request items in different rooms. The key would be to use the assessment to identify areas in need of intervention. This information would then be used to individualize programming for the student's needs.

Directly Evaluate the Procedures in Place

Practitioners should also directly test current strategies with each student to maximize their effectiveness. When evaluating procedures, teachers or practitioners should collect data on each student's performance of skills and use the data to adjust the procedures to make them more effective. This process tends to be more labor-intensive because it requires time and resources, but it can lead to more accurate and relevant information about which aspect of instruction is most effective for an individual student. For example, the following components can all dramatically influence a student's performance: style of instruction, the way a teacher or therapist behaves, or the way errors are corrected. The examples below illustrate how the effects of different aspects of instruction can be tested and evaluated with data.

Example 1—Instructor Affect

Todd has always been trained to be "fun" while working with students. He has been doing this for years, and he feels that kids like it most of the time. But when he begins working with Tyler, he struggles. Tyler seems to work well with other staff. Todd notices Tyler does his best when working with quiet staff.

Todd meets with his supervisor and decides to plan an assessment to test his interaction style with Tyler. In one condition, he interacts with high affect (loud voice, high fives); in the other condition, he interacts in a more subdued manner (quiet voice, no physical contact). They run a few work sessions (i.e., his usual discrete trial sessions) in each affect condition. Todd's supervisor measures any disruptive behavior from Tyler by counting each disruption during the session. In addition, he tracks Tyler's on-task behavior during the sessions by starting and stopping a stopwatch when Tyler is not attending to the instructor or the instructional materials. The graphs below show the differences in Tyler's behavior during the two different conditions. The dark diamonds show the rate of behavior when Todd was very animated while working with Tyler. The open (white) circles show the rate of behavior when Todd used lower affect while working with Tyler.

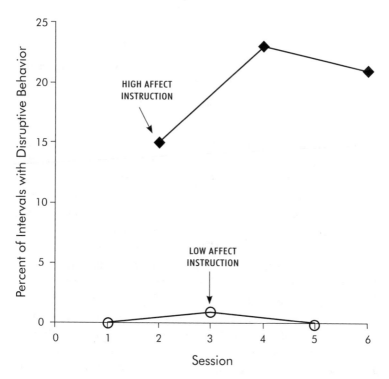

Disruptive Behavior

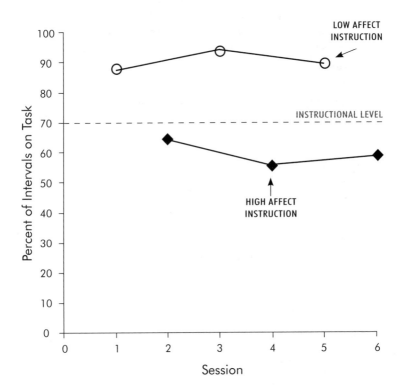

Thanks to the data and their approach to testing out the impact of instructor affect, Todd and his supervisor find that Tyler's on-task behavior is much higher and his disruptive behavior is much lower when Todd interacts with him in a more subdued manner. Based on these results, staff are trained to work with Tyler using lower-affect instruction.

It is possible that Todd and the other instructors had discussed Tyler's preferences for teaching style or other factors that might affect his behavior. Perhaps a suggestion was made that staff should work with Tyler in a certain way. What is so important in the approach Todd took to test this "theory" about instructor affect is that he and the team were able to gather evidence that clearly supported that something that they *thought* was affecting Tyler's behavior actually was having an effect. Having discussions and communicating with parents and colleagues about ways to change behavior can be much more productive with evidence and data like these, which can confirm and support a person's opinions or hypothesis about what is going on or what might happen in a particular scenario.

Let's look at another example. The following school year, Todd has the opportunity to work with another student, Caleb, in his classroom. The teacher tells him that Caleb does respond more favorably when staff interact with him in an animated manner. Based on his experience from the previous year, Todd wants to test this hypothesis to be certain that this is the case. He alternates the same two conditions (high-affect instruction and low-affect instruction) and collects data on the same variables (disruptive behavior and on-task behavior).

The graphs below show the differences in Caleb's behavior during the two different conditions. The dark diamonds show the rate of behavior when Todd was very animated while working with Caleb. The open (white) circles show the rate of behavior when Todd used lower affect while working with Caleb.

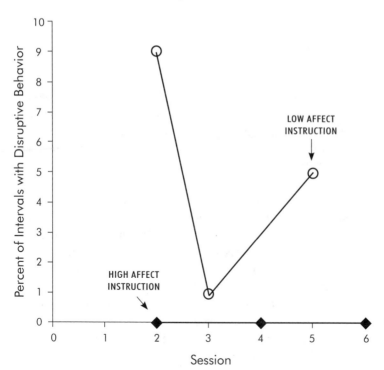

Disruptive Behavior

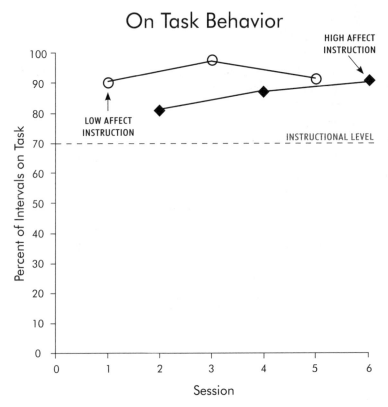

On Task Behavior

The results of the analysis show that, while Todd's affect does not seem to have a huge effect on Caleb's on-task behavior, it does seem to influence the occurrence of disruptive behavior. Caleb's disruptive behavior is considerably lower during high-affect instruction. Based on these results, staff are trained to work with Caleb using high-affect instruction.

Example 2—Types of Prompting

Ethan is a seven-year-old student with autism enrolled in a private school for children with autism spectrum disorders. When classroom staff implement academic programming for Ethan, they typically use physical guidance during new tasks to prevent him from making errors (which is common practice in many settings). However, Ethan generally does not like to be touched and will sometimes become aggressive when someone tries to guide his hands. The teacher then plans an assessment to evaluate different forms of prompting. (See more information about prompting in chapter 4, "Hands Off.")

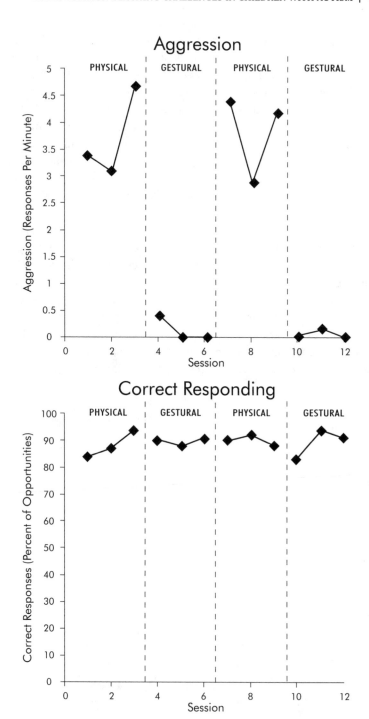

They compare two conditions: one in which they use physical prompting and another in which they use a gestural prompt (staff pointing toward the correct answer, rather than physically guiding Ethan's hand). They collect data on how often Ethan engages in aggressive behavior and the percent of the time he responds correctly.

The results of the assessment show that Ethan engages in less aggressive behavior in conditions using gestural prompting (as compared to physical guidance). In addition, the results indicate that Ethan responds correctly just as frequently in the gestural prompt condition. Based on these results, the teacher decides to change the way Ethan is prompted to a gestural prompt wherever it is appropriate.

Let's assume for a moment that the results for Ethan were a little different. Sometimes despite our best efforts, our hypotheses are wrong. Imagine the same analysis conducted for Ethan with the results depicted below.

The results of this analysis suggest that physical prompting is not what is triggering the aggression. At this point, the instructor should try to determine other variables that may be causing Ethan's aggression. For example, could it be that teachers tend to use physical prompting on new or novel tasks and that the novel tasks are the trigger for aggression?

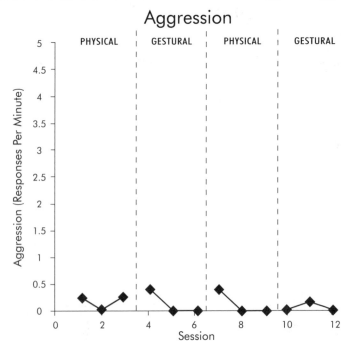

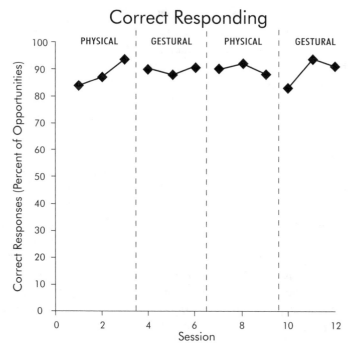

Ethan's educational team could set up a comparison to evaluate this possible explanation. Situations such as these highlight the importance of actually testing hypotheses and not assuming that one factor causes another just because the two factors appear to be correlated.

Variables to Assess

There are a number of different variables that can be assessed in addition to those in the examples above. Research has shown that there is great diversity in how individuals with autism respond to various instructional interventions. When individualizing instruction for a student with ASD, it may be important to assess how the student responds to the following variables (or others), any of which may dramatically affect how well students perform:

- the way a teacher or therapist interacts with an individual or how teachers position themselves during instruction (e.g., prompting from in front, on the side, or from behind),
- the communication modality used for instruction (e.g., picture exchange, sign language, augmentative devices),

- the use of structured or unstructured instruction (e.g., discrete trial instruction, natural environment training),
- the use of group or individual instruction,
- the use of interspersals (i.e., presenting previously learned skills during the skill acquisition session),
- the rate of instruction (rapid pace vs. slower pace)
- types of prompts used (as in the example above)
- instructor affect (as in the example above)

The prospect of evaluating all of these variables can be overwhelming. Virtually anything in the environment can influence performance. Complicating matters further is that not all of these factors have been investigated scientifically. Such factors are often idiosyncratic to specific students (e.g., they are bothered by specific sounds). To be an effective educator, teachers often need to function as detectives. Detectives typically gather information about suspects and collect evidence. Effective teachers are often required to do the same thing. They identify a variety of factors that may be causing a problem (the suspects) and they collect information that supports or refutes their hypotheses (the evidence).

Summing Up

Individuals with autism spectrum disorders, as the term implies, have skills that fall along a wide spectrum and do not all respond in the same way to different intervention strategies. Each student has a different pattern of strengths and weaknesses. Individualization allows us to identify these strengths and weaknesses and to tailor interventions to fit the needs of the students with whom we work.

Proper assessment and direct observation allow us to maximize our effectiveness when individualizing programming. The key to effective individualization is to identify the starting point for the intervention process. What proper assessment allows us to do is to identify the current level of functioning (the starting point) and then create a plan to reach a goal. Assessment and direct observation allow us to create a "road map" to reach our goals.

Effective individualization allows us to identify which strategies meet our goals efficiently and effectively. Those of us who instruct learners with ASD should intermittently step back and look at pro-

gramming goals for individuals and ask why goals are being selected. Are they selected because they are appropriate and important? Will the skill that is being taught benefit the student in five years? If we are unable to identify why a goal is being targeted or if it will be useful at some point in the future, it may be a sign of poor individualization. Goals should always be linked to long-term benefits for the student. (See chapter 8, "Make It Meaningful.")

Effective teachers are flexible in the way they provide instruction, rather than following a rigid curriculum that does not allow for individualization. While this individualization process can be a complicated endeavor, it ultimately leads to better intervention and better outcomes for the individuals and families with whom we work.

SELF-ASSESSMENT: Is Programming Sufficiently Individualized?

1. How are the student's goals selected?

   ▪ Are goals selected from a curriculum or checklist?_____

   _____

   ▪ Are assessments used? _____

   ▪ Are the results of more than one assessment compared and combined? _____

   ▪ Is parent input considered and included? _____

   _____

   ▪ Does each goal relate to both short- and long-term outcomes?_____

2. Are there clear rationales for each goal that is being implemented? For example:

   ▪ Is the skill a prerequisite for another skill or

   longer-term goal? _____

   ▪ Is it meaningful to the student? _____

3. Does each student have her own set of goals, or do most (or all) students share the same goals?_____

4. Are data being collected to evaluate the effectiveness of intervention strategies? _____

   ▪ Have different types of data been considered?_____

   _____

   ▪ Is the type of data being collected measuring the most important aspect of each skill? _____

   ▪ How frequently is the data being monitored to assess progress? _____

5. When a learner is not making the expected progress toward achieving goals, are instructional variables specifically evaluated? Examples of variables that could be evaluated for their impact on student progress include the following:

- the teacher's or therapist's style of instruction

- the teacher's or therapist's behavior

- the way errors are corrected

- the communication modality used for instruction (e.g., picture exchange, sign language, augmentative devices)

- the use of structured or unstructured instruction (e.g., discrete trial instruction, natural environment training)

- the use of group or individual instruction

- the use of interspersals (presenting previously learned skills during the skill acquisition session)

- the rate of instruction (rapid pace vs. slower pace)

- types of prompts used

_____

_____

_____

_____

8 | Make It Meaningful

Maria Arnold

Donald and Peggy Smith were excited to have their daughter, Shannon, in a quality program for children with ASD that was based on the science of applied behavior analysis. Shannon had just turned twelve when she entered her new school. She had a few words, though she didn't use words to communicate with others, nor did she use non-verbal gestures efficiently or consistently. Shannon was able to use the toilet but did not initiate the need to do so, and she did not wash and dry her hands independently. Shannon had some interest in a very narrow assortment of leisure activities that tended to have a repetitive quality (such as repeatedly pushing buttons on an alphabet book to hear the letter names), but she was unable to occupy herself for more than two minutes, according to her parents. Shannon also had some strengths, including an excellent memory for naming items (colors, shapes, letters, and numbers), the ability to sight read simple words and phrases, and precocious musical abilities such as the ability to memorize a melody after hearing it once.

It was time for Shannon's initial thirty-day assessment review after entering the program. The program staff completed both formal and informal assessments and gathered information from Don and Peggy through a parent interview and a home visit. The review would lay the foundation for Shannon's Individualized Education Program (IEP). It was clear from Don and Peggy's input that they were proud of Shannon's exceptional visual memory and musical skills, though they acknowledged her limitations in other areas. They hoped that staff would include various reading goals and artistic expression through music as part of Shannon's IEP. They were disappointed when staff proposed goals that focused on developing readiness skills (attention, responding to requests), social language, social interaction, practical skills for daily living, and sustained engagement in independent activities.

The behavior analyst explained that Shannon's good visual memory and musical talent were strengths to capitalize on in the future or to use as rewarding activities to promote task engagement. However, the educational team needed to prioritize other skills that would help Shannon care for herself and interact effectively with the people in her everyday life. In addition, the behavior analyst emphasized that focusing on the core aspects of autism now would likely help Shannon to make the most of her special talents in the future.

Shannon's therapist began to work with her on attending to her name and simple directions. The program staff used her labeling skill to expand her ability to request or mand for things she wanted. To further encourage Shannon's social initiations, they contrived situations in which others in the environment had what Shannon wanted. The more proficient Shannon became, the easier it was for her therapists to introduce new social demands. After months of work, Shannon was making more social interactions as she experienced success from the positive results of her own behavior.

Simultaneously, Shannon's educational team worked on her ability to manage her own toileting schedule using visual cues (pictures with words) that were systematically faded to just text. In this way, they were able to use a previously acquired skill (Shannon's ability to memorize words) to strengthen another skill. In addition, since toileting is a natural context for working on hygiene skills, Shannon's team embedded hygiene skills into the toileting sequence (washing and drying her hands). Though these daily living skills were not preferred activities for Shannon, upon completing her toileting and hygiene schedule, she earned time at the music center, where she and her therapist sang songs together.

The educational team also sought to increase Shannon's ability to occupy herself appropriately in leisure and daily activities for longer periods of time. Being able to entertain herself is a vital skill, as it is unlikely that her family and community will be able to provide Shannon with continuous attention now or in the future. By assessing a wide array of novel activities with which Shannon had no experience, the educational team was able to determine her interests and preferences for a greater variety of activities beyond her previous limited interests (e.g., more types of toys, technology, and repetitive tasks with a more *meaningful purpose such as recycling). The team then used the informa-tion from the preference assessment and picture/text schedules (already determined to be a useful tool) to improve Shannon's ability to sustain independent activity.*

Shannon practiced all of her skills in various contexts and with different people to help with generalization of her acquired skills. Peggy and Don were very much a part of this programming. They were rewarded by Shannon's increased ability to respond to and initi-ate interactions with family members and others, and her ability to entertain herself for longer periods of time, freeing them to do other things. In addition, Don and Peggy spent much less time in the bath-room supervising Shannon. Shannon could do a lot more now than just label colors, letters, and numbers, and entertain others with her precocious musical skills. She had developed several meaningful skills that were essential for everyday life.

Overview of the Issue: Meaningful Goals

The 1970s brought significant changes to education in the United States, especially to the service delivery system provided to children with intellectual and developmental disabilities. The 1975 Education for All Handicapped Children Act exemplified a change in public attitudes about the unethical nature of institutionalization and embraced the philosophy of normalization. This era was characterized by a progressive movement to be more accountable for what, how, and when we teach children with special needs. In the 1980s and 1990s, many educators supported mainstreaming and inclusion respectively; however, research showed that relying on a developmental curriculum that assumes children with intellectual or developmental disabilities learn the same way as their typical peers, albeit more slowly, resulted in poor outcomes for these same children (Jacobson, Mulick & Rojahn, 2007; Davis & Rehfeldt, 2006). Since then, educators have increasingly moved away from a developmental curriculum in favor of a functional curriculum that addresses individualized education to promote the development of meaningful life skills.

Meaningful skills are functional, age appropriate, and practi-cal, and they are useful now and in the future. They are pivotal skills that are prerequisites for, or components of, more complex skills, and generally promote independence, participation, and competence. Meaningful skills are skills necessary for daily living, and they promote social awareness, effective interaction, and personal responsibility. They also assist children to develop higher order skills such as comprehension, interpretation, and application of information within a social world.

Meaningful skills are skills that will be used frequently and across different environments, and they are recognized by the family and broader community as necessary and important in order for the student to comfortably integrate within her social group. They also provide access to a wider array of rewarding experiences for a learner and generally compete with inappropriate behaviors. When educators do not appropriately attend to the intent of individualized education and fail to focus instruction on the development of meaningful skills, there is a problem.

What Do Problems with Meaningful Goals Look Like?

When instructors target skills that are not immediately useful for a student with ASD, she can't benefit from opportunities to become more independent in daily life. What she is unable do for herself she will have to rely on others to do for her, creating a burden on the family and the community to provide necessary supports. In addition, the situation may set the student up to fail when she does not have the prerequisite skills to master a target skill. This delays the learning process by days, weeks, and sometimes months. It is important to be efficient on behalf of our learner by choosing meaningful goals that will be immediately useful in her daily life and increase her ability to build on the skills she already possesses.

In addition, some goals may appear "normalizing" but in fact only serve to keep a learner busy and do not effectively improve her ability to build skills that promote independence, participation, and competence. They have no immediate or future relevance for everyday life (e.g., Shannon's rote labeling skill or her ability to memorize and play any musical piece). It is essential to stay focused on what the student really needs to learn in order to successfully respond to and interact with the world in which she lives.

Where Does the Problem Come From?

There are a number of reasons why students might be learning or working on skills that are not functional or meaningful. The authors have all encountered some of the following reasons why programming is not as meaningful as it could be.

Using a Developmental Model. Sometimes parents and professionals choose goals using a developmental model. Many children with intellectual and developmental disabilities, and, in particular, children with ASD, do not follow a linear path to skill development. They do not just learn more slowly, they learn differently. A student with ASD may not work on every skill on a developmental checklist, but she should work on those skills that are building blocks for other skills. For instance, a child does not need to crawl before she learns to stand even though most children do. However, a child does need to stand before she can walk. A child's ability to attend to her environment, to use any form of language to interact with the environment, to imitate and discriminate, and to be able to care for herself are readiness skills essential in daily life. However, they are often not prioritized in favor of other less important developmental or preferred goals.

Don and Peggy derived pleasure from Shannon's ability to sing the alphabet song and label alphabet letters and simple sight words because these activities gave them a reliable form of interaction with their daughter. For this reason, they were valuable skills to them. However, Shannon's ability to sing or label for her parents was not something that was social or communicative in other settings in her life, and as she got older, these skills were not age appropriate. Spending educational time focusing on these skills did not further enhance Shannon's life the way that new social, communication, and recreational skills would.

Predetermining Goals for a Group or Level. Another deterrent to meaningful programming is for educators to have prescribed goals they teach all of their students, a practice that was discussed in chapter 7. Upon being placed in a particular class, the student is taught what the teacher teaches, and everyone is working on the same thing regardless of individual need. The child may then spend time working on skills she has already mastered, on complex skills for which she has no prerequisites, or on skills that do not appreciably improve her ability to respond or act on her own behalf on a daily basis. This makes it all the more important to develop an appropriate individualized education program based on assessment of the learner's immediate and future needs.

Not Considering Both Formal and Informal Assessment in Choosing Meaningful Goals. Formal assessments are important tools that inform decision making, but they may also obscure our understanding of what are truly meaningful skills for a student, and compromise the outcome for her development. For instance, when employing normative assessments such as the Battelle Developmental Inventory (BDI, Jean Newborg, 2004) a teacher may determine that a child does not demonstrate several skills in all five domains of the inventory. These results, however, do not help the teacher determine which skills are a priority. Educators and caregivers may simply start from the earliest missing skill in each domain, or inappropriately implement programming for every skill the child is missing. This can result in delays in more meaningful skill development, or in reduced learning opportunities for the child due to overloaded instructional programming.

Information derived from formal assessments must be put into perspective. Again, educators and caregivers should consider both current and future needs when developing individualized education plans. This may require an *ecological assessment*—an in-depth observation of a learner's daily routines, the environments in which she spends time, as well as a survey of the family's long-term plans for their child. This assessment should address questions such as the following:

- Can she communicate her needs and wants, and if so, where and how?
- What can she do for herself?
- What supports does she need throughout her day?
- Can she tolerate "no" or the need to "wait?"
- What motivates her to interact with others?
- What are her special interests?
- In what environments does she demonstrate the greatest variety of skills?
- In what environment is she most uncomfortable, unengaged, or anxious?
- What vocational aspirations does the family have for her?
- How will she spend her leisure time as an adult?
- What skills and supports will she need to attain positive outcomes?

So, while assessments are important tools to assist in decision making, data derived from formal assessments do not always capture the "whole picture." Educators and caregivers must consider the "whole picture" when determining what is most meaningful for the learner. They should also keep in mind that it is not the number of skills in each category of a developmental inventory that a child acquires that is important, but the quality of the acquired skills she demonstrates consistently in the act of daily living.

Failure to Put the Student's Needs First. Another deterrent to the implementation of meaningful goals is the educator's susceptibility to the desires and pressures of concerned parents and other caregivers. Teachers and behavior analysts are often the initial authors of individualized programming for students with autism spectrum disorders. While parents and other caregivers make important contributions to the educational process, there may be disagreements about what is most important or meaningful for a student. Professionals, parents, and other caregivers must strive to maintain an educational partnership without compromising accountability to the learner by always putting her needs first. Taking the time to discuss and define the concept of what makes goals meaningful may help ensure greater agreement or more effective compromise when there is disagreement.

Why Is It Important to Recognize the Problem?

Children with autism spectrum disorders require intensive and focused programming to achieve meaningful gains. They often need more time to acquire skills than their typical peers. If we dilute educational programming with goals that do not have obvious meaningful outcomes, or attempt to accomplish too much at once, we reduce the number of learning opportunities for more functional goals and contribute to delayed acquisition of these goals. In addition, spending time on nonfunctional goals limits the learner's opportunities to practice functional skills she has acquired in order to maintain and generalize these skills.

It is important for educators, parents, and other caregivers to recognize the challenge of determining meaningful skills and the importance of assessment data and direct observation of daily routines as part of the process. This information is more likely to help professionals and caregivers choose meaningful skills that are immediately important to the learner, and to choose skills that will serve as building blocks for other later developing skills. Professionals and caregivers also must be sensitive to their own biases in order to put the learner's needs first. Educational programs that are driven by parental pressure or that rigidly pre-prescribe learning by developmental level or some other fixed criteria do not support meaningful, individualized education.

In Shannon's case, the behavior analyst prioritized joint attention, requesting, and responding to others. A person who learns to attend (listen) to a speaker, respond to a speaker, and make requests using a consistent means of communication (sign, pictures, or verbal) will more readily access what brings her pleasure than a person who simply labels items in the environment. She is using language in a more meaningful way to get what she really wants. This, in turn, is likely to lead to increased interaction with her environment and even build a broader vocabulary as she is introduced to a wider array of things she likes.

Shannon's behavior analyst also focused on improving her ability to engage in independent activities for longer periods of time, and to manage her own personal needs consistently, at home, at school, and in the community. These are all practical skills of daily living, and building blocks for more complex skills for the future. Letter and number labeling, broadening Shannon's sight word vocabulary, and her artistic expression became peripheral goals, which, in isolation, were irrelevant; however, the behavior analyst wisely incorporated these into functional programming and used them to motivate Shannon.

What Can We Do about the Problem?

Parents and educators should evaluate what they know about students using assessments (both normative and criterion based), surveys, and direct observation before determining new goals and objectives for them. They must first identify skills a student has within specific domains such as social communication, skills for daily living, cognitive skills, health and safety, physical fitness and recreation, and vocational skills, as well as her level of independence and competence for each, and the various contexts within which she uses these skills. This will then help parents and educators distinguish skills that are necessary from those that are not, those that are building blocks for other skills, and those that will need to be carried over for refinement, maintenance, and generalization.

Ask the Right Questions to Determine Meaningful Goals. Once we have a good understanding about what a student can do, we can begin to determine new annual goals and objectives for her by asking important questions about skills we *think* may be important. For instance, educators and caregivers may ask the following questions:

Is it meaningful?	YES / NO	RATIONALE
1. If the learner can't do it, will someone else have to?		
2. Is the skill age-appropriate for the learner?		
3. Is the skill needed immediately?		
4. Will it continue to be needed in the future?		
5. Is the skill needed frequently?		
6. Will the skill be needed in multiple environments?		
7. Can it be maintained by naturally occurring events?		
8. Does the learner's family/ community value the skill?		
9. Does the learner have the prerequisites to learn the skill?		
10. Does the skill promote independence or hinder it?		
11. Will the skill provide access to new reinforcers for the learner and compete with inappropriate behaviors?		
12. Will the skill promote participation by the learner?		

These and other questions are discussed in more depth in the body of work of Louis Brown and his colleagues (Brown, Nietupski & Hamre-Nietupski, 1976).

Consult Appropriate Resources. Educators and parents can turn to a variety of resources to assist them in identifying meaningful goals. For instance, *Essential for Living* (McGreevy, Fry & Cornwall, 2012) is a teaching manual with information on communication, behavior, and functional skills assessment, curriculum, and skill-tracking. In this resource, the authors provide a step-by-step assessment and decision-making tool as well as instructional strategies for teaching functional skills to children with special needs. Their scope and sequence chart prompts professionals and caregivers to consider whether a proposed skill is "nice to have, good to have, should have, or a must have."

Other sources may include tools such as the Assessment of Functional Living Skills (by Partington and Mueller) or a curriculum developed with functional skills in mind, such as the Core Skills Assessment component of the ACE (Autism Curriculum Encyclopedia). There are also a variety of technological resources such as various apps for the Apple iPad and VizZle from Monarch Teaching Technologies, which is a web-based program that can be used to support and motivate students, as well as to serve as a source of easily accessible (downloadable) materials such as picture schedules, visual cues, and instructional videos. These are just a few examples of resources which may be able to provide a starting point for parents and teachers to think about goal development.

Focus on Useful Foundation Skills. Educators and parents also should focus on building pivotal skills, beginning with immediately useful, basic, and simple skills that will provide a strong foundation upon which to build more complex skills. Then, following this, they should systematically add more complex skills as the student progresses, doing so in a very deliberate way.

Practice Skills in Meaningful Contexts. In addition to determining skills needed now and in the future, educators, parents, and other caregivers should take the time to identify meaningful contexts in which skills should be taught based on where the skills will be used now and in the future. Students with ASD struggle with generalization, so we should not assume that skills taught in simulated contexts will generalize to the real world. Students with autism are most likely to achieve the best outcomes when they are taught and practice skills in current and future environments in which they live, recreate, socialize, work, or volunteer.

Individualize Teaching Methods. Educators and caregivers should think about how each skill will be taught and what we know about a child that will assist in developing effective and meaningful programming. It is helpful to build on previously acquired skills and use an individual's choices and preferences when developing individualized instructional strategies. Some may need a very structured model such as discrete trial training to develop basic skills, but others may not prosper in this teacher-directed format and may learn more and faster within a more natural context. This information needs to be carefully considered and balanced to ensure that children are benefiting from the type of instruction that is most effective while also learning to benefit from different types of instruction and settings as appropriate. Specifically *testing* questions such as these using the methods described in chapter 7 will help ensure that data are being used to guide these decisions.

Monitor Progress by Taking Data. Another way to address the problem of identifying and promoting meaningful skill development is to monitor the decisions we make through data. For instance, let's think about Shannon. Suppose that at baseline (initial level), using percent of opportunity data (the number of times Shannon demonstrated her need to use the toilet divided by the total number of opportunities to indicate her need to use the toilet), Shannon's ability to indicate her need to use the toilet was 0 percent in all settings. After six months of instruction using visual supports such as a picture schedule, an augmentative communication system, and systematic instruction in a variety of natural contexts, Shannon was able to indicate her need to use the bathroom 65 percent of all opportunities at home and in school. The data show that her programming is effective and has had a positive, meaningful effect on her life—her ability to initiate interactions with others and act on her own behalf. The data suggest we stay the course.

However, perhaps we review Shannon's ability to wash and dry her hands when the need occurs incidentally within her hygiene schedule. Using a task analysis, we determine that at baseline, Shannon completed only 20 percent of a ten-step sequence independently. After two months, Shannon still only completes 20 to 30 percent of the ten-step sequence for washing and drying hands independently when given multiple opportunities throughout her day. The data suggest that Shannon may need a different model of instruction to make more meaningful progress. We can also use data to help determine which instructional method helps Shannon makes the most progress in the shortest period of time.

Summing Up

In conclusion, the process of educating children with autism spectrum disorders or any disability should be directly linked to the assessment and identification of meaningful skill development for the individual. Research suggests that focusing on practical or functional skills promotes the most positive long-term outcomes (Wehman & Kregel, 1997, 2001). As educators and caregivers, we have a responsibility to assess what is meaningful to individual learners, what the deterrents to meaningful programming may be, and how we can address them. Furthermore, we need to access all available resources to support meaningful skill development, use those resources as best we can, and continuously monitor the choices we have made and the efficacy of our instructional strategies on behalf of the students we teach.

SELF-ASSESSMENT: Are You "Making It Meaningful"?

Observe teaching interactions within the classroom and respond to the following questions:

1. What skills are being targeted for the student?

_____

_____

_____

2. How will these skills be used in the learner's daily life?

_____

_____

_____

3. Once the student acquires the targeted skill, will it provide access to new reinforcers? _____

_____

 ■ What are those reinforcers? _____

_____

_____

 ■ How will the skill provide access to them? _____

_____

_____

4. Does the targeted skill have social validity? In what way?

_____

_____

5. Is the target skill a prerequisite or a component of a more complex response? If so, which one?

_____

_____

6. Does the targeted skill complete with inappropriate responses?
   If so, which one(s)? _____

   _____

7. Is there any concern that the targeted skill:

   ■ Is not needed in the learner's daily life? _____

   ■ Hinders independence? _____

   ■ Is busy work? _____

   ■ Cannot be completed because of missing prerequisite skills?
     If so, what prerequisite skills are needed? _____

     _____

     _____

References

Ahearn, W. H., MacDonald, R. P. F., Graff, R. B., & Dube, W. V. (2007). Behavior analytic teaching procedures: Basic principles, empirically derived practices. In P. Sturmey & A. Fitzer (Eds.), *Autism spectrum disorders: Applied behavior analysis, evidence, and practice* (pp. 31–83). Austin, TX: Pro-Ed.

Anderson, S. R., Avery, D. L., DiPietro, E. K., & Edwards, G. L. (1987). Intensive home-based early intervention with autistic children. *Education & Treatment of Children.*

Birnbrauer, J. S. and Leach, D. J. (1993). The Murdoch Early Intervention Program after 2 years. *Behaviour Change, 10,* 63–74.

Brown, L., Branston, M. B., Hamre-Nietupski, A., Pumpian, I., Certo, N., & Gruenewald, L. (1979). A strategy for developing chronological age-appropriate and functional curricular content for severely handicapped adolescents and young adults. *Journal of Special Education, 13,* 81–90.

Brown, L., Falvey, M., Pumpian, I., Baumgart, D., Nisbet, J., Ford, A., Schroeder, J., & Loomis, R. (1980). *Curricular strategies for teaching severely handicapped students functional skills in school and non-school environments* (Vol. X). Madison: MMSD.

Brown, L., Nietupski, J., & Hamre-Nietupski, S. (1976). The criterion of ultimate functioning. In M. A. Thomas (Ed.), *Hey, don't forget about me: New directions for serving the handicapped* (pp. 2–15). Reston, VA: Council for Exceptional Children.

Charlop, M. H., Schreibman, L., & Thibodeau, M. G. (1985). Increasing spontaneous verbal responding in autistic children using a time delay procedure. *Journal of Applied Behavior Analysis, 18,* 155–166.

Cooper, J. O., Heron, T. E., & Heward, W. L. (2007). *Applied behavior analysis.* Upper Saddle River, NJ: Pearson/Merrill-Prentice Hall.

Davis, P. K., & Rehfeldt, R. A. (2007). Functional skills training for people with intellectual and developmental disabilities. In *Handbook of intellectual and developmental disabilities* (pp. 581–599). New York: Springer US.

Davis, P. K., & Rehfeldt, R.A. (2006). Functional skills training for people with intellectual and developmental disabilities. In J.W. Jacobson, J.A. Mulick, & J. Rojahn (Eds.), *Handbook of intellectual and developmental disabilities* (pp. 581–599). New York: Springer.

Delmolino, L., & Harris, S. L. (2012). Matching children on the autism spectrum to classrooms: A guide for parents and professionals. *Journal of Autism and Developmental Disorders, 42,* 1197–1204.

Dickson, C. A., MacDonald, R. P. F., Mansfield, R., Guilhardi, P., Johnson, C., & Ahearn, W. H. (2014). Social validation of the New England Center for Children-Core Skills Assessment. *Journal of Autism and Developmental Disorders, 44,* 65–74

Dube, W. V., McDonald, S. J., McIlvane, W. J., & Mackay, H. A. (1991). Constructed-response matching to sample and spelling instruction. *Journal of Applied Behavior Analysis, 24,* 305–317.

Dunn, L. M., & Dunn, L. M. (1996). *Peabody picture vocabulary test.* Circle Pines, MN: American Guidance Service.

Eldevik, S., Hastings, R. P., Hughes, J. C., Jahr, E., Eikeseth, S., & Cross, S. (2009). Meta-analysis of early intensive behavioral intervention for children with autism. *Journal of Clinical Child & Adolescent Psychology, 38*(3), 439–450.

Foxx, R. M. (1982). *Increasing behaviors of severely retarded and autistic individuals.* Champaign, IL: Research Press.

Green, G. (2001). Behavior analytic instruction for learners with autism: Advances in stimulus control technology. *Focus on Autism and Other Developmental Disabilities, 16*(2), 72–85.

Grow, L. & LeBlanc, L. (2012). Best practice recommendations for teaching receptive identification to children with autism. *Behavior Analysis in Practice, 6*(1), 56–75.

Ingersoll, B. (2008). The social role of imitation in autism: Implications for the treatment of imitation deficits. *Infants & Young Children, 21*, 107–119.

Iwata, B. A., Dorsey, M. F., Slifer, K. J., Bauman, K. E., & Richman, G. S. (1994). Toward a functional analysis of self injury. *Journal of Applied Behavior Analysis, 27*(2), 197–209. (Reprinted from *Analysis and Intervention in Developmental Disabilities, 2*, 3–20, 1982).

Jacobson, J., Mulick, J., & Rojahn, J. (2007). *Intellectual and developmental disabilities.* New York: Springer.

Kazdin, A. E. (2013). *Behavior modification in applied settings.* Long Grove, IL: Waveland Press.

Krantz, P. J., & McClannahan, L. E. (1993). Teaching children with autism to initiate to peers: Effects of a script fading procedure. *Journal of Applied Behavior Analysis, 26*, 121–132.

Leaf, R., McEachin, J., & Taubman, M. (2012). *A work in progress companion series, Volume 2: Learning how to learn.* New York: DRL Books.

Leaf, R. L., & McEachin, J. (1999) *A work in progress: Behavior management strategies and a curriculum for intensive behavioral treatment of autism.* New York: DRL Books.

Lovaas, O. I. (1987). Behavioral treatment and normal educational and intellectual functioning in young autistic children. *Journal of Consulting and Clinical Psychology, 55*(1), 3.

MacDuff, G. S., Krantz, P. J., & McClannahan, L. E. (1993). Teaching children with autism to use photographic activity schedules: Maintenance and generalization of complex response chains. *Journal of Applied Behavior Analysis, 26,* 89–97.

Maurice, C. E., Green, G. E., & Luce, S. C. (1996). *Behavioral intervention for young children with autism: A manual for parents and professionals.* Austin, TX: Pro-Ed.

McGreevy, P., Fry, T., & Cornwall, C. (2012). *Essential for living: A communication, behavior, and functional skills assessment, curriculum, and teaching manual for children and adults with moderate-to-severe disabilities.* Orlando, FL: Behavior Change.

Miltenberger, R. G. (2011). *Behavior modification: Principles and procedures.* Boston: Cengage Learning.

Newborg, J. (2004). *Battelle developmental inventory.* Itasca, IL: Riverside Publishing.

Oren, T. (1999). Early childhood special education. In B. T. Ogeltree, M. A. Fischer, & J. B. Schultz (Eds.), *Bridging the family-professional gap: Facilitating interdisciplinary services for children with disabilities* (pp. 164–182). Springfield, IL: Charles C. Thomas.

Partington, J. W. (2008). *The Assessment of Basic Language and Learning Skills-Revised (The ABLLS-R).* Pleasant Hill, CA: Behavior Analysts.

Partington, J. W., & Mueller, M. M. (2012). *AFLS: The assessment of functional living skills.* Marietta, GA: Stimulus Publications.

Sarakoff, R. A., & Sturmey, P. (2004). The effects of behavioral skills training on staff implementation of discrete-trial teaching. *Journal of Applied Behavior Analysis, 37,* 353–358.

Sheinkopf, S. J., & Siegel, B. (1998). Home-based behavioral treatment of young children with autism. *Journal of Autism and Developmental Disorders, 28* (1), 15–23.

Skinner, B. F. (1957). *Verbal behavior.* New York: Appleton-Century-Crofts.

Stokes, T. F., & Baer, D. M. (1977). An implicit technology of generalization. *Journal of Applied Behavior Analysis, 10,* 349–367.

Sundberg, M. L., & Partington, J. W. (1998). *Teaching language to children with autism and other developmental disabilities.* Pleasant Hill, CA: Behavior Analysts.

Sundberg, M. L. (2008). *VB-MAPP: Verbal Behavior Milestones Assessment and Placement Program: A language and social skills assessment program for children with autism or other developmental disabilities: Guide.* Concord, CA: AVB Press.

Tarbox, R. S., Wallace, M. D., Penrod, B., & Tarbox, J. (2007). Effects of three-step prompting on compliance with caregiver requests. *Journal of Applied Behavior Analysis, 40,* 703–706.

Tullis, C. A., Cannella-Malone, H. I., Basbigill, A. R., Yeager, A., Fleming, C. V., Payne, D., & Wu, P. F. (2011). Review of the choice and preference assessment literature for individuals with severe to profound disabilities. *Education and Training in Autism and Developmental Disabilities, 46*(4), 576.

Wehman, P., & Kregel, J. (Eds.). (1997). *Functional curriculum for elementary, middle, and secondary age students with special needs.* Austin, TX: Pro-Ed.

Appendix A
An Overview of Preference Assessments

The information below is reprinted, with permission, from *Incentives for Change: Motivating People with Autism Spectrum Disorders to Learn and Gain Independence* by Lara Delmolino and Sandra L. Harris (2004).

Assessing Your Child's Interests

A number of clinicians and researchers in the field have developed special assessments to help identify preferences in individuals who may not spontaneously demonstrate interest in a range of items. These assessments involve setting up specific environments and choices, and then carefully observing a child's behavior under different conditions. Watching a child's behavior can give clues about new items or activities that may be reinforcing. These assessments are also important to consider when reevaluating a child's preferences. As we know, a child's preferences and interests change over time, and even from moment to moment. Borrowing strategies from these assessments and even conducting mini-assessments on a frequent basis can help a parent or teacher to be aware of new and changing interests for the child. However, these assessments do take time. If your child has many clear preferences, you may not wish to pursue this process. On the other hand, if you are hard pressed to find potential reinforcers, it will be worth the effort.

The Pace Method

One type of assessment was developed by a group of researchers led by Dr. Gary Pace (Pace, Ivancic, Edwards, Iwata, & Page, 1985). In this assessment, a set of sixteen possible items is first identified by people who are familiar with the child and her behavior. The items to be tested may include things the child has previously shown an interest in on other occasions. The items may also be novel materials, or may be new items that have some characteristics that might interest a specific child. For example, if your child has shown an interest in brightly colored objects and often brings objects to her eyes while playing with them, toys or objects such as prisms, kaleidoscopes, or colored sunglasses might be introduced. Typically, items chosen should be relatively easy to present to a child and practical to use as a reinforcer.

The sixteen items are then divided into four groups of four items each. The assessment is conducted over eight sessions. Each session assesses one of the groups of four items, and each group is assessed in two separate sessions. In the first session, a teacher or parent presents the child with one item at a time and records whether the child "approaches" or plays with the item. If she does, she is allowed to play with it for a few seconds. If the child does not interact with the item, the instructor might gently prompt her to touch or hold the item, or activate it to show the child how it works. The child is then given another chance to approach the item on her own.

After presenting the first item, the instructor goes through the other three items the same way. Next, he or she presents all four items one at a time again, but in a different order, with only one item visible at a time. During each session, the child is exposed to the four items in one group five times. By the time all eight sessions are finished, the child has been able to try each of the sixteen items ten times.

The instructor takes careful data to keep track of whether the child approaches the item on her own during those ten trials. The most preferred items would be those that she approached the greatest percentage of times. For example, if a child reaches for and plays with the spinning top eight out of the ten times it is presented to her, it would have a score of 80 percent. Dr. Pace and his colleagues showed that items that were approached 80 percent or more of the time were very likely to be effective as reinforcers. The table below shows sample data for a group of four items using the Pace procedure.

Sample Data for an Assessment Based on the Pace Procedure

Group 1	Trial 1	Trial 2	Trial 3	Trial 4	Trial 5	Trial 6	Trial 7	Trial 8	Trial 9	Trial 10
	Session 1					Session 2				
Prism	A P	A P	A	A P	A P	A P	A P	A	A P	A
	R	R	R	R	R	R	R	R	R	R P
	P+	P+	P+ P	P+	P+	P+	P+	P+ P	P+	P+
	P-	P-	P-	P-	P-	P-	P-	P-	P-	P-
Top	A P	A P	A	A P	A	A P	A P	A P	A P	A P
	R	R	R	R	R P	R	R	R	R	R
	P+	P+	P+ P	P+	P+	P+	P+	P+	P+	P+
	P-	P-	P-	P-	P-	P-	P-	P-	P-	P-
Licorice	A	A	A	A P	A	A P	A	A P	A	A
	R	R	R	R	R P	R	R	R	R	R
	P+ P	P+ P	P+ P	P+	P+	P+	P+ P	P+	P+	P+ P
	P-	P-	P-	P-	P-	P-	P-	P-	P- P	P-
Play-doh	A	A	A	A P	A P	A	A	A P	A	A P
	R	R P	R	R	R	R	R	R	R	R
	P+	P+	P+ P	P+	P+	P+ P	P+ P	P+	P+ P	P+
	P- P	P-	P-	P-	P-	P-	P-	P-	P-	P-

A = Approach, R = Reject, P+ = Approach after prompting, P- = Reject after prompting

The Pace stimulus preference procedure is a systematic way to introduce new items to your child that may be potential reinforcers. This is especially useful for children who may not naturally show interest in a variety of different items. Of course, you will not know if a particular item will act as a reinforcer until you see that it can effectively increase behavior. And, as we learned before, the item may not be a reinforcer at a specific moment in time if there is no Establishing Operation (EO) in effect....

The Fisher Method

Other procedures in addition to the Pace method have been developed in order to assess a child's preference for items and to determine how reinforcing each item is compared to other items. For example, your child may like crackers, but crackers are no competition for cookies! So, while the Pace procedure can help identify what new things your child might like, another procedure can be helpful to determine which things your child might like more than others.

One assessment of this type was designed by a group of researchers led by Dr. Wayne Fisher (Fisher, Piazza, Bowman, Hagopian, Owen,

& Slevin, 1992). In this assessment, sixteen items are identified in the same manner as in the Pace procedure described above. A grid is established in which each item is paired with another item to be tested. The grid is arranged so that every possible combination of items can be assessed, for a total of 120 pairs. The child is presented with a pair of items, and an observer records which item the child reaches for or manipulates out of the pair. There is no need to ask the child what she wants—the choices can be presented without the use of language, which is an advantage when working with a child who has limited language. If the child does not show any interest in either object, the clinician might demonstrate each object's use or give the child a sample of each item before presenting the pair again.

Based on the percentage of times a particular object is chosen, the items can be rated in a general order of preference. So, although you might already know that your child likes bubbles, books, and cars, using the Fisher procedure you can find out whether any of these items are chosen more than others. For example, you can offer her bubbles and a wind-up car and see which she chooses. Then offer bubbles and a book, and finally the book and the car. Note that you do not need to use sixteen items to follow this procedure. See the sample data sheet below for an example of what results might look like with just four items (instead of all sixteen).

Sample Data for an Assessment Based on Fisher's Procedure			
☑ Bubbles	☐ Car	☐ Car	☑ Book
☐ Bubbles	☑ Book	☑ Car	☐ Popcorn
☑ Bubbles	☐ Popcorn	☑ Book	☐ Popcorn
Bubbles chosen 2/3 times = 66% Book chosen 3/3 times = 100% Car chosen 1/3 times = 33% Popcorn chosen 0/3 times = 0%			

The DeLeon and Iwata Procedure

Other researchers, Drs. Iser DeLeon and Brian Iwata (1996), designed an alternate method of systematically assessing an individual's preferences. In this model, a child is presented with an array of seven items that may be interesting or appealing. She is asked to select one item from the group. Each time she demonstrates interest in an item, she is allowed to play with or manipulate it for a brief period. After that, the object is removed and the order of the remaining objects is rearranged. The child is then asked to choose again, and the procedure is repeated until all items are gone. After the child has chosen all of the items, the session is completed.

Later that same day or on another day, all seven items are presented to the child again. The entire procedure is repeated for a total of five sessions, with no more than one or two sessions per day.

After completing this assessment, you will have information about the items that were chosen first and last in order to make some comparisons and predictions about the possible strength of some items as reinforcers. For example, if your child selects a whistle first in all five sessions, the whistle might be a very strong reinforcer for her. On the other hand, if she takes a wind-up toy last (seventh) in four out of five sessions, then it may be a weaker reinforcer. The following table gives an example of possible data using DeLeon and Iwata's procedure.

Sample Data for an Assessment Based on DeLeon & Iwata's Procedure							
	Wind-up toy	Hand held fan	Rubber ball	Reflective sticker	Graham crackers	Oreos	Whistle
Trial 1	7th	5th	6th	4th	3rd	2nd	1st
Trial 2	7th	6th	5th	4th	2nd	3rd	1st
Trial 3	7th	4th	6th	5th	3rd	2nd	1st
Trial 4	5th	6th	7th	4th	3rd	2nd	1st
Trial 5	7th	5th	6th	2nd	4th	3rd	1st
Average	6.6	5.2	6	3.8	3	2.4	1

Some Considerations in Assessing Your Child

With all these procedures, it is important to remember that compiling a list of items your child enjoys and "ranking" these in order of preference does not guarantee that these items will be effective as reinforcers and capable of motivating behavior at any given moment. Have you ever heard a teacher say that a child "just won't work for any of her reinforcers" or that a child "is not motivated by any of her rewards?" We know that not all pleasurable activities are motivating at all times. What delights us one day may have less appeal the next. What makes a particular item a reinforcer at a specific point in time is the EO (establishing operation).

Identifying a list of your child's preferences is therefore just a *first step* in being able to motivate her to engage in important behaviors. If a teacher identifies a list of preferences and stops there, she is likely to run into problems, as we described above, when the reinforcers don't work. However, having a longer list of possibilities will be helpful, because if some potential rewards don't seem to be working as reinforcers, others may. Understanding the EO allows us to learn more about when a preference is established as a reinforcer and when it is not, and, by definition, when it will work to motivate behavior, and when it will not. We will learn more about using EOs to our advantage in later chapters.

You may run into a number of challenges when trying to set up and conduct reinforcer assessments with your child. For example, what if your child seems completely disinterested or won't participate or attend to the assessment procedure itself? There are a few different things to consider in this case. First, you may need to examine the items that you have selected to use in your reinforcer assessment and see whether you need to include different items that will better capture your child's attention and interest. You may also need to consider the setting where you are assessing your child. The room or space you are using may be too large or too distracting, and a smaller environment might be easier to begin with. Also, you may be able to adjust the format of the assessment. For instance, it is not necessary for your child to sit at a desk or table to participate. Items may be placed on tables, in bins, or on the floor, and your child can approach the items she wants. This way, a preference assessment can be conducted for a child even if she does not sit down and readily attend to an instructor.

Sometimes it may be difficult to find a pattern when looking at the data about which items your child chose. If so, it might not seem that she has clear preferences. Then again, if she has chosen many of the items, it may be that she has a wide range of interests, or enjoys novelty. This is important and helpful information that can be used when working to motivate your child. If your child has many interests or is interested in novel items, it will be helpful to use a large number of frequently changing items as reinforcement.

For the purposes of a preference assessment, it is not important that your child play with the toy or object in any particular or "correct" way. The goal of these procedures is to find out what she likes to do. If she prefers to play with a certain item in a potentially dangerous way or some other unacceptable way, you would probably choose not to use this item to motivate or reinforce your child's behavior, and you probably would not include such items in the assessments. For other items, you may want to weigh both the advantages and disadvantages of using an item your child "plays" with in an idiosyncratic way. For example, your child may choose to play with a book nine out of ten times it is presented, but plays with the book by repeatedly fanning the pages, rather than reading or looking at the pictures. In this case, the book is still considered a strong preference for your child. It is up to you to decide whether you are comfortable with using books as one of the ways to motivate your child. In the early stages of teaching, you may be willing to compromise by allowing some of this atypical behavior to help motivate your child to learn new skills. Once new skills have been established, it may be easier to find newer or more "appropriate" reinforcers.

Appendix B
Quick Reference Guide:
Eight Essential Teaching Strategies

This appendix presents each of the strategies covered in this book in outline form so that you can use the summaries as quick reference guides.

1. Make It Worthwhile
2. Don't Give It Away
3. Wait for It
4. Hands Off
5. Talk Less
6. Quality over Quantity
7. Individualize
8. Make It Meaningful

1: Make It Worthwhile

What do we mean?
- Is the learner motivated to learn or participate in the lesson?

What does the problem look like?
- Student does not engage with any items
- An item or activity seems to motivate or hold the learner's attention briefly, but then loses potency
- Student will select item, then doesn't seem to want it
- Nothing competes with stereotyped behavior

Where does the problem come from?
- Assuming preference—this worked last time so…
- Ways we are determining preference: just because student approaches an item doesn't mean it's a reinforcer
- Habituation to items we have—using same items over and over again
- Too much free access
- Too much effort to get item (not worth it)

Why is this a problem?
- In order for there to be reinforcement of skills, there has to be motivation for the reinforcer
- Not establishing proper motivation will lead to lack of progress with programs, off-task or inappropriate behavior, overreliance on response prompts for compliance

What can we do about the problem?
- Get better at finding reinforcers: watch what the student does; channel to more appropriate behavior
- Be creative or inventive: introduce novel items or creative ways to interact with items
- Stack the deck in favor of appropriate behavior regarding quality, quantity schedule, duration, delay
- Avoid ratio strain: balance amount of work to reinforcer access

2: Don't Give It Away

What do we mean?
- Find a balance

What does the problem look like?
- Extended periods of "mand training" where mands are not really being "trained" because the student already knows *how* to mand
- Ongoing pairing "sessions"—important to establish aspects of instruction and instructor as conditioned reinforcement, but when is it time to move beyond reinforcement for "being there?"
  - Do we ever check to see if pairing has occurred?
  - How would we do that?
  - The importance of distinguishing between lack of pairing and lack of motivation

Where did the problem come from?
- Criticism of earlier teaching models (e.g., DTI), overuse of negative reinforcement (i.e., "Do what I ask and then go play")
- Influx of "Verbal Behavior" programming
- Increased focus on learner initiation
- Desire to create a motivating work environment and establish ourselves as conditioned reinforcement

Why is this a problem?
- We end up creating "mand" vs. "no-mand" time: other salient cues in the environment, preferred items, positioning
- Satiation before work begins! (Why work for it when I get it for free, or at least for just asking, if this is a learned skill)
- It goes on too long—within a work session and over time

What can we do about the problem?
- Think long term (big picture)—What is the learner's history?
- Focus on building compliance—by rewarding naturally occurring/high probability responses, but not "behavioral momentum" at lightning speed
- Be aware of other cues
- Remember—reinforcement should be available DURING work, not just BEFORE work, but it does not have to be included explicitly in every schedule

3: Wait for It!

What do we mean?
- If they aren't looking, they aren't attending

What does the problem look like?
- Student reaches toward materials before the instruction (SD) is delivered
- Student does not make eye contact while the instructor is delivering the instruction
- Student looks up at lights while handed materials to match
- Student reaches toward/grabs preferred item while turning away from the instructor
- Instructor is taking data while delivering an instruction

Where did the problem come from?
- Teaching language, social, and academic skills before teaching "how to learn"
- Delivering reinforcement without pausing or teaching the student to make eye contact with the instructor for feedback after responding
- Delivering reinforcement while the student is engaged in off-task behavior
- Presenting the instruction without establishing appropriate attending/eye contact

Why is this a problem?
- Variable attending skills/eye contact: attending to preferred stimuli instead of relevant stimuli; not attending to relevant stimuli
- Difficulty in shifting attention from one stimulus to another
- Attending to vocal instruction/instructor in the presence of visual stimuli
- Difficulty attending in situations where there are multiple stimuli, such as scanning, tracking visual stimuli, eye contact with instructor in a small group, eye contact with peers in a small group

What can we do about the problem?

- Focus on "learning to learn" skills:
  - attending to the speaker's voice by orienting to the speaker; responding to hearing his own name (eye contact/look at the speaker)
  - Waiting quietly for a direction to be given
  - Making eye contact with the speaker
  - Listening to teacher instructions
  - Waiting quietly and making eye contact with the instructor for feedback (corrective or reinforcement)

4: Hands Off!

What do we mean?
- Examining the role of physical guidance in teaching

What does the problem look like?
- Hand-over-hand guidance when:
  - the student is not oriented/attending to the task
  - the student has previously demonstrated the task independently
  - the student is not motivated to respond/is noncompliant

Where did the problem come from?
- "Working through" noncompliance
- Physical prompting as a behavior plan, not a teaching strategy
- Unsure of what else you can do if there is insufficient motivation
- Student gets the message "You can do it yourself" or "I can help you"
- Because physical contact serves to orient the learner
- Because no other prompts work

Why is this a problem?
- Many learners are passive recipients of physical prompting, not learning
- If used often, future responding may improve after use of physical prompts following errors
- It may become a punishment (a consequence that a learner will seek to avoid)
- Reliance on physical prompting may reduce our likelihood of exploring different motivation
- Learners get bigger
- It looks unnatural
- It can lead to behavior problems
- It produces a short-term result over a long-term result

What can we do about the problem?
- Stop and think before physically prompting

- Determine what will be accomplished: learning compliance or learning a skill?
- Teach responding to other prompts (gestures, pointing, modeling)
- Never prompt a basic response that is in the student's repertoire, such as touching or pointing to target stimuli. Remember: if they know *how* to point to something, they just may not know *what* to point to, or they may not be motivated

5: Talk Less!

What do we mean?
- The role of language in teaching

What does the problem sound like?
- "Charlie Brown teacher"
- Extra language to make demands seem contextual
- Classroom and school "catch phrases"
- Nicknames
- Run-on sentences during inter-trial intervals

Where did it come from?
- Fast-paced use of interspersals
- Language as filler when taking data/preparing for next trial
- Desire to make tasks functional and contextual
- Classroom culture develops in every school!

Why is this a problem?
- Language that is beyond learner comprehension is used
- Learners are less likely to attend to us
- Teacher instructions and praise become less salient
- It creates a loud, distracting classroom environment

What can we do about the problem?
- Be aware of your learner
- Pause between praise and giving the next instruction (SD)
- Be cautious of unnecessary SDs
- Use simple and salient SDs, not unnatural SDs
- For older learners, move from simple to natural instructions
- Save your personality for the reinforcement!

6: Quality over Quantity

What do we mean?
- Focusing on how much instruction is provided, rather than on the quality of the learning experiences and interactions

What does the problem look like?
- Delivering instructions when the learner is not ready to learn
- Focusing on a minimum number of learning opportunities, sometimes at the expense of quality opportunities
- Focusing on rate of instruction, which can affect quality
- Presenting isolated learning opportunities rather than contextual ones

Where did the problem come from?
- Focus on fast pace
- Teaching using interspersals
- Need for a minimum number of learning opportunities to convert data to a percentage
- Focus on staff behavior over student outcome

Why is this a problem?
- Some students we are trying to teach are not ready to learn
- Some learners require an unnatural pace in order to comply with demands
- We spend more time teaching skills than necessary
- Students aren't always able to generalize skills to more natural contexts

What can we do about the problem?
- Focus on preparing our learners to learn
- Provide more meaningful opportunities
- Move away from seeing "more" as the only measure of quality
- Spend more time planning for higher quality opportunities
- Consider alternatives for data collection

7: Individualize!

What do we mean?
- Individualization is important, but it is challenging to actually make happen
- Individualization may mean individualized relative to typically functioning students (but like all of the other ASD students), or each student has a unique program tailored to his or her specific needs and assessments are conducted to individualize programming

What does the problem look like?
- Many students with the exact same goals, even if the goal doesn't make sense for a particular student (e.g., every student in a classroom has the same envelope-stuffing goal)
- Rules designed for a specific student get used with another even when there is no rationale for doing so (e.g., we use an error correction with Timmy and it works, so we should use it for all of the students in our class)

Where did the problem come from?
- Earlier models of ABA service
- Habit ("I've been doing this effectively for years now; why change anything?")
- Cost efficiency: it is easy to do, less training required for staff, materials are present
- Certain procedures are adopted and implemented globally without allowing the literature to "catch up"

Why is this a problem?
- Just because a type of intervention strategy works well with some of our students does not necessarily mean it works for all students
- Delivering services and education that are not individualized results in poorer outcomes for students.
- It also results in lower quality training
- There is more than one way to get from A to B

What can we do about the problem

- Conduct assessments to make sure we are using the best possible instruction procedures given the situation (error correction, affect, interspersals, communication modality)
- Identify the things that set the occasion for learning
- Find a balance: too little individualization vs. too much individualization
- Complicated does not mean individualized!

8: Make It Meaningful

What do we mean?
- Meaningful target skills are functional and should provide students with access to new reinforcers, have social validity, promote *generativeness* (facilitate subsequent learning by either a prerequisite or a component of a more complex response), and compete with inappropriate responses

What does the problem look like?
- Targeting skills that student doesn't need in his or her daily life
- Targeting skills that hinder independence
- Targeting skills that the student does not have the prerequisites to complete
- Working on skills that function as busy work

Where did the problem come from?
- Goals determined by age or similar classroom programs rather than individualization and need
- Assessments in the absence of seeing the big picture or developing long-term goals
- Parent requests or pressure

Why is this a problem?
- Students with ASD require intensive and focused programming to achieve meaningful gains
- Focusing on nonfunctional programming takes time away from functional programming
- Sets the student up for problems with acquisition and maintenance

What can we do about the problem?
- Determine what supports the student will need in adulthood
- Determine what skills he or she needs to gain the most independence
- Ask how will the student use this skill in daily life?
- Each program we implement should keep long-term goals in mind

Contributors

Maria Arnold is Director of Educational Services at the Douglass Developmental Disabilities Center. She holds a master's degree in special education with certification as a teacher/supervisor, and is a board certified behavior analyst. Maria has participated in program development, administrative leadership, supervision, and training within the autism community for nearly forty years.

Lara Delmolino is a board certified behavior analyst and holds her Ph.D. in clinical psychology from Rutgers, the State University of New Jersey. She is a Clinical Associate Professor at the Graduate School of Applied and Professional Psychology and Director of the Douglass Developmental Disabilities Center.

Kate Fiske is the Associate Director of Behavioral and Research Services at the Douglass Developmental Disabilities Center, and a Clinical Assistant Professor at the Graduate School of Applied and Professional Psychology of Rutgers. She holds a doctoral degree in clinical psychology and board certification in behavior analysis. She has been providing assessment and treatment to individuals with ASD for sixteen years.

Catriona Francis is an Assistant Director of the school program at the Douglass Developmental Disabilities Center. She is a certified teacher of students with disabilities and holds a master's degree in educational administration. She is a board certified behavior analyst who has been providing training to teachers working with individuals with ASD for twelve years.

Robert H. LaRue is a Clinical Associate Professor at the Graduate School of Applied and Professional Psychology at Rutgers. He earned a dual doctorate in biological and school psychology from Louisiana State University in 2002. He has worked with individuals with disabilities for over twenty years.

Debra Paone is the Assistant Director of Outreach Services at Douglass Developmental Disabilities Center. She holds a Ph.D. in behavior analysis/learning processes from the City University of New York at Queens College. She has been working with individuals with ASD using the principles of applied behavior analysis for twenty years.

Kimberly Sloman is an Associate Director of Behavioral and Research Services at the Douglass Developmental Disabilities Center, and a Clinical Assistant Professor at the Graduate School of Applied and Professional Psychology at Rutgers University. She holds a Ph.D. in psychology, and has been working with individuals with ASD for fourteen years.

Benjamin R. Thomas is Associate Clinical Director of the Claremont Autism Center at Claremont McKenna College, and a board certified behavior analyst. He holds a master's in psychology with an emphasis in behavior analysis from Queens College (CUNY), and is completing his doctorate in developmental and child clinical psychology at Claremont Graduate University. He has over fourteen years experience providing service and training to individuals with developmental disabilities, their educators, and their families, in a variety of settings.

Index